Choking God

AKA

You Get To Keep the Shoes

Richard Carlston
Copyright © 2024
All rights reserved.

All rights reserved. No part of this publication may be reproduced, distributed, or transmitted in any form or by any means, including photocopying, recording, or other electronic or mechanical methods, without the author's prior written permission, except in the case of brief quotations embodied in critical reviews and certain other non-commercial uses permitted by copyright law. For permission requests, please get in touch with the author.

Contents

Acknowledgments i

About the Author ii

1: A gun, a shovel, slaughter, and transformation ... 1

2: Coy forty-fives and hippopotamuses 17

3: Finding room for gluttonous hoop skirts 33

4: Garfunkelish epiphanies and fake throws 40

5: Overshadowing, is not a free-will event 48

6: Ode to Theseus 67

7: Sisyphus meets Don Quixote 79

8: So, who is this God, literally? 105

9: "For answer, see other side." 117

10: Hippos swallow snakes, swallowing hippos . 131

11: Sackcloth and ashes 147

12: Eating Timothy 152

13: Death, birth, resurrection. And an assault rifle 157

14: The first real space cowboys. Or, turning vegetation into jubilation 175

15: 'Sailing on that Silvery Mist.' Copulating with my own vulnerability 194

16: Scouring the stick of life for one last everlasting tootsie savor 217

17: "Eloi, Eloi, lama sabachthani?" 232

18: Firewalking and masters of illusion 244

19: Salvation, and my nose in his glory's belly ... 259

20: *Le roi mourra*. Or, love my enemy, …kill him if necessary 271

21: A gun, a shovel, and the alphabet soup 286

22: You get to keep the shoes 290

Acknowledgments

I wish to thank my father, a man of letters, who instilled in me a love of books. My Religious teachers, for teaching what they thought was best, without which teachings, my muses may have been silent. I thank my daughters, for entreating me with their lives and examples.

Thank you, David, Mark, Doug, Dan, Jacqueline, Terence, Shasta, Driele, Josie, Sebastian, and my friends who encouraged me to write.

About the Author

Transformation may often be a result of those who seek it. Gaining from, and sometimes leaving behind, the teachers and the monsters in one's life. This work, while perhaps seeming to tread liberally on cherished beliefs held by others, is, rather, this author's own wrestle within this author's personal journey. The author wishes to thank all of the monsters and teachers, who willingly, and sometimes unwillingly, participated in this journey.

1

A gun, a shovel, slaughter, and transformation.

It's difficult to put a finger on just exactly what caused me to sleep with a loaded Mack-90 assault rifle outside my bedroom door. After all, this was the 90's, no pun intended. I'm not a violent person. Including the time I smashed Tom's head with a gallon jug of purified water. That was anger, not violence. I wanted to put him out of *my* misery. Ten pounds of water was the closest object I could find that wouldn't kill him. Only later, would I think how easily I could have broken his neck with that blow. God knows I wanted to. Fortunately, God knows I'm not a violent person. Unfortunately, I don't believe in God. Not naked. Not choking a man to death in the desert in his own spit. Besides, I didn't have a shovel long enough, to dig a hole deep enough, to bury him, and his car, his girlfriend, and all the others who he had terrorized back into their cars and tents. My friends could wake me in the morning for pancakes.

•••

"DRINK ME," Alice read.
And so she did, unquestioningly.

That's why I don't believe in God anymore. I'm a believer of small print.

'No known side effects,' the god-makers say...

> Warning! May cause war, crusades, rape, bigotry, hatred, Inquisitions, torture, racism, and mob mentality.

•••

Years ago, my friend Ben had the shit pummeled and kicked out of him by a priest and two retired Christian missionaries in the name of ...small print.

'DRINK ME,' their God said. 'My blood will make you clean from the blood and sins of this generation.'

I bet they were humming the small print of the Te Deum when they broke Ben's sleeping body. Weeks later, Ben described to me through a wired jaw that the police had also found bloody footprints on his front door. It had been kicked in for a second time that night as these self-determined emissaries of God apparently felt they had not finished their message.

I recall the biblical Passover. The 'small print' reads, "take blood... and strike it... on the door posts. And when I see the blood, I will pass over you...and not suffer the destroyer to come in your houses to smite you."
Oh, excuse me, Mr. kind, loving God, but my friend Ben could not pick himself up from the bedroom floor with broken ribs, cheek bones, nose, and jaw...will his own blood do?
I shudder, and I remember the night I visited Ben after he was released from the hospital. Ben removed for me from a plastic bag the 'robe' that had been his bed sheet. It was caked with dried bloody shoeprints.

Passover?

Really?

No blood on the doorpost for all those annihilated Egyptian baby boys? Slaughter the sleeping innocents. Destroy their innocent lives. What brilliant 'works' from these benevolent gods. Use the children as bait; their Gods bade. Invite them, perhaps, on a sacrificial hike. Prepare to have a roast. Demand the child to carry their own wood. And while they are at it, to build their own altar. Say to that child, "Oops, no lambie." And this child's very own father will, unquestioningly, step forward to cut the child's heart. Let mighty works of wonder drown out the "But Daddy, Daddy," while voices of 'Gods' ring in the heads of the sacrificers.

I wonder if Hitler and these 'Gods' had the same voices in their heads? I wonder if I should even be wondering that? The total impunity. "Kill the children of the heathen." "Burn their parents." "Obliterate every man, woman, and child."

"Fee Fi Fo Fum… crush their bones to make my bread."

"But I will be your God, and you will be my people."

Jehovah and Hitler counting piles of gold. Plundered from the Egyptians in a mythically awkward exodus. Then spoiled back from the plunderers, in yet another horribly awful exodus. Men, women, and children, were laid asunder, picked, and plundered. The now familiar voices in the heads of the sacrificers. Claiming. Choosing. Purifying.

And for what? To make little angelic golden "cherubim" sit on either side of these deluded god's 'mercy seats?.' And what the hell does this 'mercy seat' mean between two cherubs anyway? Oh! It's to remind me how merciful these terrible gods have been to anyone who does not believe the way they do. You know. Weeping. Wailing. Gnashing of teeth. That is... gnashing teeth that have all their gold fillings yanked out first. "Let my people go." Of course, after they plunder your storehouses.

Mercy?

Passover?

What in the name of these Gods inspires people to slaughter? Not everyday slaughter like warfare, murder, starvation. I mean, what inspires a people, 'in the name of their Gods', to slaughter? Read their holy books, and you'll have holy wars, crusades, inquisitions, occupations, Muslims, Christians, Jews, prophets, priests, and believers, all slaughtering "gentiles" and each other, in the name of their jealous gods.

I clobbered Tom in the name of his God. With my friends watching, I smashed him to the ground and screamed my disgust into his face.

●●●

Putting reason aside for that evening, Tom had over-stimulated his Aquarius mind into thinking it had been 'outed' before its time. He had become both ecstatic and angry in a careless rage, with some sort of religious twist to it. Then he began shouting about how I was some sort of god or something. "You knew." "You knew." He would rant over and over. "How did you know?" "You did this for ME?" "For ME?" …he would shout, on and on and on. Sometimes even kneeling at my feet in what felt like a theatrical mockery of the God he was addressing.

Something that evening had triggered him to go off in his aggressive, out-of-control behavior. Eventually, it was enough for him to freak out all the others, who then left the Solstitial bonfire for the safety of their tents and cars. Was he having a reaction to something right there, in the middle of the desert? And then it would start all over again.

"Do you know who you are?"

He would demand to know. Grabbing my arm as if to make me answer. And, since I really didn't know *who* I supposedly was to him, I could only, at best, play along. With the wrong answers. Hoping he wouldn't get more violent.

I had been introduced to Tom by Alisha, my retired actress friend who was also there on that trip. She was part of a group of friends that came together in the new age of the early nineties while attending some esoteric Bailey lectures. Her Patrician character reminded me of Ginger on Gilligan's Island, while describing circular Pavlovian axioms, being and nothingness, form and the formless, thoughts preceding matter, with that trademark elocution

Being born in the fifties, on the afternoon of the last day of the fifties, to be exact, I was barely old enough for the sixties. While technicolor was bringing new life to heroes and heroines being chased by giants on the big screen, I was also running from giants that had *me* pressed up against the big screen, big fence, small town, pants down, knees shaking, body aching, mind racing, chest facing, Zodiac Killer. But more about that later.

Tom was a familiar name in the community. I had attended one of his opening shows at an art gallery where I was later introduced to him by Alisha. As well as being a good artist, he also taught relationship courses at a state college and on radio talk shows. Sometime later, I ran into him at an outdoor music event. Tom had heard through the grapevine about a road trip to the desert that I had planned with a group of my friends for the summer solstice. This group was a ménage of budding new agers who met each other over the years on quests for 'holy grails.' Some had met through lectures, others through retreats and workshops. We all knew each other well enough to spend three days in the desert together, except for Tom. Tom had been the only exception.

It quickly went from bad, to worse. Tom was in the dementia of a psycho-religio-epiphany, and seemed incapable of reeling himself back in. He had become the human equivalent of a mad-dog. Nothing mattered anymore. He had apparently, right then in the middle of the desert, decided to *be* in his 'heaven.' No judgment day. No pearly gates. No Peter. No confession. NOTHING mattered now. Not a metal camp chair, thrown at Dave and Shelly's Chevy van. Not another metal chair crushed like an axe into great grandma Marilyn's silver tray, a family heirloom upon which had been served some of our evening feast. Not handfuls of sand, thrown into our only jugs of drinking water, miles into the desert. Not…

"Fuck!" Fuck!" Fuck!"

…yelled at the top of his lungs relentlessly for hours. Then he got even more angry. He got angry at all of us for being in **his** Heaven without telling **him** about it sooner.

"You knew."
"You knew."

… he would yell, in an accusatory way, as if we had cheated him by excluding him from the apparent circle of initiates. This particular group of friends had been together on many previous desert trips. It wasn't unusual for some or all of us to spend these warm summer desert evenings dancing to music and shrooming around our immense fires.
Each fire would take on its own personality. Logs too heavy to lift would be rolled onto the fire by several people. Each pyre became an intimate relationship. The intense heat and crackling chaos demanded our attention, awe, and careful tending. Each evening began with everyone in the camp gathering the wood that

would burn through the night. The piles of trees and branches would often reach the height of a pick-up truck.

Bacchanalian confections and libations transformed and liberated individuals, often obliterating the delicate balance of agreements that usually lend permanence, commitment, and restraint to mutually bound relationships. A sense of jubilation, perhaps heightened by our indifference to clothing, distilled our inhibitions. Each night was a beautiful process. The Pan-like nature of the fire tempting out of us our thoughts and expressions. Pushing on the boundaries that we brought with us from our busy-bee lifestyles, while at the same time defining values around which new boundaries would be essential.

This unusual shamanic cacophony of nakedness and hedonism was shattered as Tom 'came out' before us. He looked like a devil as his demon paced the heat of the fire. His foaming mouth was interrupted by his throat screaming obscenities.

"Fuck you, Katie!"

… he screamed at his non-consensual shaman psychologist, as if she were present. I felt the urge to find a weapon. A jawbone.

A sling. Something. Most of the others moved away to their tents not far away and, by now, were freaked out by the whole specter. Tom was clearly much larger than me. He was naked, crazed up, and ranting his cause to his invisible god as if he were angry at himself for having been unnecessarily diligent, only to find that his god had let the rest of us into his heaven by some imaginary back door. Alisha approached him to calm him down, but he cuffed her in the throat with his hand as if to shut her up. The next instant, he shoved Mari over a fallen log…
So, I BECAME his 'God.' In all His furious, jealous power.

•••

The phone rang. It was Ben, calling me from the hospital after his beating. I visited him later that same day. As I listened to the details of Ben's ordeal with his assailants, my stomach tightened. I felt like puking my anger and third-person rage all over Ben's self-proclaimed 'Christian' perpetrators. Through a straw, he sucked the rest of his pureed lunch into his now-wired jaw. While we walked back to his hospital room, I listened to his thoughts on forgiveness…

"What would Christ do?" … he asked.

I wanted to **scream,**

"For Christ's sake, look what they did …. in Christ's name!"

Fortunately, I don't believe in Gods.

•••

I had been taught that God was jealous, God was vengeful, and that he visited judgement on the unjust. I'd had enough of all three to know *he* wasn't going to fight any of my battles for me. I loaded the Mac-90 and placed it against the wall outside my bedroom door. As I rested my head next to the barrel of the gun, I decided to love my enemy, or kill him if necessary.

•••

I was given the assault rifle in the early nineties by a friend I met at an offshoot branch of Werner Erhard's EST. Group transformation in a neat little box, literally. The Zen masters cane temporarily changing lives. Mystic grottos of mass seclusion. Mistaken grotesqueness of mass illusion.
For that brief moment in time, the transformative doors of my new age were

open, and I stepped in. I wasn't searching. For God, anyway. Someone had given a friend of mine the five-hundred bucks needed to pay her way for a transformational three-day training, behind closed doors till four in the morning, hugging total strangers. I was searching for what the hell went on with my friend behind closed doors till four in the morning, in total secrecy. I did find what I was searching for. But I can't tell you. It's "against the rules."

Transformation, like 'happily ever after,' is a rip. I really just wanted the solution to sex, money, and happiness. Instead, I found myself beating on a chair, chanting, 'I want to be loved.' That seemed to be the right answer; I could move on to the next level. Money and happiness were the only 'issues' that needed processing.

'God is love.'

Now don't you forget that. And the bible tells me he might love *his* wife, or he might love *yours*. Luke called it, 'overshadowing.' It *is* a little overshadowing, isn't it?
Oh, and excuse the bastard child.

All in all, I did get transformation. Fifteen-hundred-dollars worth of it. Put me in a bubble, give me a social lobotomy and voila! I'm transformed. I know. I've been there before. Only I call it tripping. They call it transformation. Equally as temporary. Exactly as misleading. It feels like getting laid. Love is dripping off everything. Forgiveness is. Because everything is cool. And everybody loves everybody. Love flows like water. My thoughts are both interesting and senseless at the same time. I become like Mickey in Fantasia with the wizard's hat on. Commanding all the brooms and buckets that I can imagine. The river Jordan is getting full, and I'm about to dive in.

Then, just as willingly as I fall into the rabbit-hole of transformation, I must, as unwillingly, exit. Out through the in- door. The ship doesn't just come in. It also goes out. With the tide. In and out. A very natural process. And it is not my hat. It is The Wizards. After all, didn't I just happen to find it where the Wizard left it? Of course! After I've paid my fifteen-hundred dollars. Taken my oneness pill. After I've followed my next messianic 'transformation' fad. All just wizard, priest, or pope-dominated pit stops in this ever-mutating, evolving, beautiful thing I know as life.

So, naturally, **those** hats belong to the pit-stop Wizards. The storytellers. I've found

that I have to carry my own water, to my own baptism. Fill the font with my own bathwater. Then let out the drain afterwards.
I will remember to let out the drain, won't I?

Even if someone told me that I could stay in the warm bathwater all day? Day after day. Week after week. Eating fruit from all the trees in the garden. Warm water. Naked. Not ashamed. Swimming in love and oneness.
"Oh, that one I'll call Goat." "That one I'll call Lamb." "That one I'll call Swine." "That one I'll call Eve." "That one can be Adam, the Tin Man." Brooms will carry warm water. As much of it as I want. For as long as I want. And it will last forever. And it will be a New Age…in cinematic oneness.
Yea, right. Then reason floats me an apple, and I reach out to grab it with a prune, that looks like a hand, pretending to be a prune.

I've found that love, faith, positive mental attitude, transformation, affirmation, hope, belief, and trust are just mentally induced 'pit-stops' in this thing called life. Each one is dominated by its own promise-producing wizard. And by little casino-boss mentalisms that advertise the 'loosest slots.' That pay out ninety-seven percent on all the emotional tokens that I willingly play through their looking glass. Each crackpot jackpot belief then adding up to just subtly less than I had gambled, and substantially more delusion as I coast in, to the next pit-stop wizard. Follow my next rabbit-hole, belief. Over and over.

2

Coy forty-fives and hippopotamuses.

You know, 'a dog is a man's best friend.' I suppose a 'good dog' is even *that* much better of a friend. Have you seen how a dog will chase its own tail for hours? Hoping to run fast enough to catch up to it? Repeatedly hoping.

I have some 'good dogs' in my psyche. Tails I chase. Repeatedly hoping I'll catch. Yet somewhere deep inside, knowing I won't. Ever. Kind of like that 'between' place where I *knew* the mystery of Santa, Jesus, and the Tooth Fairy, but I still believed. For the benefits, of course. Presents. Friends. A shiny new quarter.

Take Natalie, a cute neighbor of mine, for example. She'll ask me to do a favor. And you know, with a smile on her face, she could get me to do anything,
….well, almost anything.

For the real dirty work, she would need to smile AND do her coy little 'forty-five.' You know, that forty-five-degree head-tilt to the side that implies, if done just so, (to the perspective of the honey-doer), "I'll do anything if you'll do this for me…please?"

That's the beauty of the 'forty-five.' Like the great mystery of godliness. It gets the job done. Yet, it has never technically guaranteed anything. I've been a real sucker for this one. And it works every time. Kind of like throwing a stick for a playful dog. Into the lake. Into the bushes. Even the fake throw. The dog will do anything just to play.
I'm not saying I'm a dog, but even though I've figured out these 'forty-fivers' in life you watch, they will still work almost every time. Just watch me follow the rabbit…. I mean the stick…. I mean the smile…. I mean the 'forty-five.' Like a good dog. Exactly *not* like a hippopotamus.

The benefit I hope to get is hidden in *my* understanding of the 'coy-forty-five.' My expectations of the myth. *My* understanding and trust in my friends, teachers, parents, gods, priests, lovers. *My* apparent willingness to allow the 'house' to win. Always.
Can you imagine what would happen if Santa only delivered empty boxes? Each neatly wrapped in 'coy-forty-five' paper? Implied gift giving? Be good little boys and girls. Really, really good. Climb up on my knee. Ask Santa for *anything* you want. Watch

Mommy and Daddy sweat. Ho, Ho, Ho. Kind of funny, isn't it?
That is, until little Johnny-be-good climbs up. Searching Santa's eyes for a miracle. Placing a worn photograph into Santa's hand. "I want my dog Sam to come back for Christmas." Ho, Ho, Ho. Kind of funny, isn't it? Are you still laughing? Life is like a big fat bowl full of jelly. Isn't it? Not really.
You see, man's best friend took me behind the curtain of the great and powerful OZ, and I only found a little gray-haired man. Trying to pull off another coy-forty-five. The saddest fairytale ever. And while I was still dreaming, I saw hope, trust, love, forgiveness, the golden rule, Jesus, and Santa all take to the sky behind eight tiny reindeer and one big fat "I'm sorry." Cut loose in a convenient sandbag, of course. The moral of the story?

Believe. Believe. Believe.

You get to keep the shoes. Spit shined for your next conundrum.

Did you know the hippopotamus is just a fish out of water? They are really quite nimble swimmers. Yet, you'd never guess it. They are the kings of poker faces. Try playing toss the stick with a hippo. Give them your best please-coated 'forty-five.' Promise that you won't do any fake throws. See if they'll roll over for a biscuit, or for a grassy savannah with a lagoon in hippo heaven. Damned pessimists. Nonbelievers. You won't see them in a circus. It's called discretion. A strong constitution. Solid, man.

When I chase missive forty-fivers in life, illusionary promises, I am also like a fish out of water. Not in my element. Nailing my *self* to a cross with every ambivalent 'omni hope.' Every effervescent good intention. Literally gambling my life away with every trusted face card. Minimizing my own returns. Not improving my own humanity.

The moral of this lesson for me has been to 'be like the hippo.' Think 'hippo love.' 'Hippo agreements.' 'Hippo friendships.' Hippo anything. Solid, man. Steady. Discretion. Reason.
Exactly, *not* like a dog.

Dogs wouldn't make good gamblers. Living at the beck and call of their master. Fake throws. A hippo would not be writing my story. A hippo would have been listening discretely with its tiny little ears from the back row during the Sunday sermons of my childhood.

CHOKING GOD

●●●

Back to the dogs. I also have some 'bad dogs' in my psyche. Bones, I have not let go. These are not man's best friends. Yet these I also chase religiously. 'Woofing' and twitching in my sleep. Licking my own wounds. Tasting the blood. Down to the bone. For the benefits, of course.
A fistful of gleaming vital organs pulled fresh out of the steaming carcass of a redeemed "it's O.K.," or a repented "I forgive you."
Pit stop wizards, whatever.

While anger sleeps
Forgiveness weeps
Big tears of confusion
Psychic delusion
Pissing on nails
That press thick flesh
Onto sagging crosses
That redistribute the losses
Of 'silent' killings
As even thoughts provoke
A sacrifice or two
Shedding layers
Of politely placed
"It's O.K.'s"
And
"What are you thinking about"?

"Nothings."
Till pain comes rapping, tapping
On twisted nerves
And bent 'remembers'
Offering them candies
And sweet nothings
If they'll just take a ride'
Come in and abide
With the 'nice' stranger
Of forgiveness
That paints passing lanes
Around hurts and pains
And violent deeds
Speeding off toward signs
Of congestion, indigestion
Loves erection
Pinking, shrinking
Into limp-dick-fruit-of-the-womb
Under-panted traffic jams
B A M !!!
"Thinking about **everything**"
Comes rear-ending loves ass
"It's O.K.s"
Screaming "it's not"!
Skidding, kidding themselves
Into thinking it ever was
SLAM, SLAM, SLAM
"Not O.K's"
Confronting
Rear
End of forgiveness

CHOKING GOD

Bloody pieces of "I'm Sorry"
"It's O.K.," "I forgive you's"
Tossed around on the ground
Around other pieces of
Faked verbal orgasm
Politically polite persuasion police
Wrap yellow streamer bandages
Around the event of who hit whom
First, or is it last?
The Sinaic black or white referee god
Deciding who's O.K.
And who's not
Untwisting nerves and bent remembers
To tow away loves car
Loves scar remaining fixed
Beneath layers of Bondo "it's O.K." cream
The tires good for another kick or two
Like new, slightly used want ads
Peddling "runs like a charm"
Candy wrapped forgiveness machines
Dragging wrecked angle rear-ends
Into pat-on-the-back conversations
About what's O.K. and what's not
Greed's erection sticking its self
Into Faith's pockets
As, "it's A-O.K.s"
And "anything wrong with it?"
…"Nothings"
Pull nails out of crosses
To redistribute the losses
Of another sacrifice or two

And while forgiveness sleeps
Anger reaps big tears of derision
Frantic collision
Psychic collusion
Cyclic illusions
Of what's O.K., and what's not
The black and blue referee god
Makes lists of ten
Again and again
Offering candies and sweet nothings
Bending 'remembers' into twisted nerves
Nice strangers in passing lanes
Saying "it's O.K." "It's O.K."
Rapping, tapping loves erection
Into fruit of the womb traffic jams
Violent deeds
It's not O.K., it's not O.K.
It's not
O.K.?
And forgiveness weeps
While silence keeps
Pissing on nails
Of another sacrifice or two

●●●

What are my thoughts on forgiveness? Excuse me for my cynicism. But Ben, aren't you sucking your lunch through your wired jaw with a straw? Does letting things go, forgiving, or saying things are O.K. really improve your humanity in any way? Or do you just end up tormenting yourself when days later you feel like screaming "That's not O.K.?"

In the end, I found that my trust in religion, faith, God, love, or my self-proclaimed transformation each gave me exactly less than I had expected, like the little casino bosses. Exactly, *not* improving my humanity. Less is not more. Expectation sucks. Literally. Having faith in something sucks. Literally. Pays back only ninety-seven percent.
I saw my friend Ben literally suck his lunch into his forgiving, wired jaw. Perhaps nature was subtly telling Ben to keep his mouth shut. To not forgive. To let his perpetrators live with the unforgiven aftereffects of their unimproving deeds. To preserve exactly one hundred percent of his humanity. His 'self.' No saviors. No losers. No body on a cross.
Good Lord! Get me a nail, for Christ's sake.

•••

Have you ever heard the saying, 'Power corrupts. Absolute power corrupts absolutely?' Absolute anything corrupts. Absolute rightness. Absolute leftness.

Absolute monotheists with their absolute dogmas.

'Absoluteness' by its nature will eventually breed indifference or contempt. 'Absolute' waddles around like a gluttonous fat queen screaming "off with their heads" to all her contemptible, familiar unfortunates. Just take a look around you. Absolute religions with their absolute truths. Absolute believers in their absolute gods. Absolute people. All, trying to bend nature into a square. Fold the natural world into soulless, origami, Adams and Eves.

•••

What in the name of God inspires people to slaughter? Absolute power? Absolute belief in gods? Absolutely controlling dogmas? Absolutely chosen believers? What inspired three men to pummel the shit out of my friend Ben? Absolute power? Absolute jealousy? Absolute frenzy to control lovers? What did it look like?

Well, while a zealous messenger of Christ's 'Good News' was out delivering his message of peace to the people of the world, his 'origami' lover Jennifer, back in his hometown, had decided to fall in love with my friend Ben. Ben equally fell in love with her. Meanwhile, the messenger of good news returned from his evangelic mission to heathen lands to find that his lover had unfolded her origami wings and had 'naturally selected' my friend Ben. Ben and Jennifer were 'head over heels' in love.

With their marriage imminent, the retired evangelist unleashed his jealous furry by spying on the soon-to-be betrothed couple. Not unlike God, as the story goes, unleashing his jealous power on the soon-to-be betrothed Mary and Joseph, eventually "overshadowing" Mary with his absolute lust.

Well, one evening, while being spied upon, Ben and Jennifer were found to be in the stable. In other words, Jennifer was found privately spending a late evening at Ben's home. Both were unaware of the 'Charlie Manson' that was developing outside in the absolute mind of the veteran Christian Soldier.

Now, this soldier was no ordinary soldier. He had read his bible. Especially the parts where women have been dignified as God's little play things. Pawns for sodomites. Pawns for posterity. Pawns for his sanctioned polygamous patriarchs. He had *not* read the part where Jesus asked absolute moralists to

"cast the first stone." To pause their senseless momentum for a moment.
Like most good Christians, really, really good Christians, this veteran knew that nothing 'right' goes on between lovers after eleven o'clock at night. So, he had decided it was his 'God given,' lust-driven duty to start gathering stones. Gather accusers.

He began by gathering Jennifer's father, who was a priest by devotion and a doctor by vocation, telling him that his first-born daughter had been 'spied' spending late hours at Ben's home, and that 'this or that' was certainly happening right then as they were speaking. On his next late-night call, he gathered Jennifer's two brothers. Both ex-football players, and both of them also ex-evangelic missionaries. So, let me see, that's one Christian-soldier-spy-for-Jesus, two recently retired evangelic Christian missionaries, all brothers no less of 'Gods virgin', and one Christian priest father.
How obedient! How righteous! He had amassed an army of god-fearing, message-of-peace-bearing, little-Charlie-Mansonites, by one o'clock in the morning of that fateful night. All ready and willing to cast the first stone.

So, meanwhile back at the stable, Ben had been well into his slumber when Jennifer had stopped in for a visit. She told him that she felt like staying for a while to talk about their betrothal plans. Ben told her he had early morning meetings and that he needed to get to bed early. Jennifer dozed off next to Ben, delaying her drive home a while.

Their message was swift and deliberate. Without warning, the 'army' had kicked in the front door to Ben's home. They tore Jennifer's clothed, sleeping body from Ben's side, then proceeded to liberally kick, stomp, and pummel Ben's sleeping hundred-and-eighty-pound, California-state wrestler body. The screaming and hysterical Jennifer was forced outside where she could not interfere with the carnage. In male-dominated Christianity, she is just a 'pawn' after all. Why should her own priestly father and Christian missionary brothers trust her screams declaring they hadn't 'slept' together? That they should leave Ben alone?

God is lust, remember? Absolute lust. Corrupting absolutely. 'Overshadowing' someone else has never been a free will experience for that person.

At some point, the carnage stopped. The 'blood of Christ' had saved (lusted) another soul. There were no more 'first stones' to cast. But wait, the bloody finger of God had not yet written its message on the wall. So, returning moments later, the diligent band of Christian soldiers kicked-in the entrance a second time, which explained the bloody footprints police had found on door. The army had returned to finish its message....

"Mene, mene.... "

"A time to hate...A time to kill."

You know the rest.

By the time Ben's neighbors were awakened by the commotion, the perpetrators had already left with their captive pawn. Ben had managed to crawl into the bathroom, where he was found propped against the closed door to protect his damaged body.

Great is the mystery of godliness. Ben ended up settling out of court for damages. (In order to preserve the goodly reputation of Jennifer's father). He also ended up getting married to Jennifer. He also ended up forgiving his accusers, including paying back the entire out-of-court settlement. True forgiveness does not keep the spoils of war. Doesn't watch the blame mantras do their annihilation. True forgiveness 'bears its cross.' For a reward in heaven.

Meanwhile, retired missionaries and priestly doctors can go on with their condoned, unscarred reputations. Malpractice insurance in the name of the 'Forgiveness Umbrella Plan.'

That's why forgiveness is a lie. A pretension of benevolence, smothered in subliminal sublime paybacks.

"I forgive you"… cha-ching.

"Oh, it doesn't matter"… cha-ching.

Rewards stacking up in a mythical heaven, cha-ching, cha-ching. Greedy little bastards. We're all in it for the rewards. Theists and atheists alike. Building earthly mansions here, building heavenly mansions there. You've heard the saying, "The have's, and the have not's." I say "the have's, and the will have's." Those that have (here, now) family, friends, wealth, possessions, the physical reality of their mental agility. And those that (in their believing minds) 'will have,' someday, the glorious eventuality of their moral proclivity.

3

Finding room for gluttonous hoop skirts.

I was raised in a family where the belief was taught that the world revolved around a god. "The" God. Who, along with Jesus, saints, and all the prophets, knew what was best for all mankind. (Of course, hidden under the gluttonous fat skirt of a convenient ecclesiastical benefactor).

"Father knows best," meant God The Father.

Being right was something that would always happen 'later,' in heaven. That is, if I were good enough, obedient enough, to a god I've never seen. Maybe then, I would get into that heaven where my rewards for good deeds were stacking up. Like a healthy woodpile right next to my heavenly mansion. We were taught to not 'lay up treasures on earth,'
And, to make sure that we weren't cheating, our ecclesiastical 'big brother' was right there to make sure that our hearts were non-existent here on earth. That is to say, that we were to have no treasure, or no vainglory, here on earth. And, therefore, no heart.

"Where our treasure was …(in heaven),

There our heart would be also."

Do all good unto others. This life is just but a moment. Certainly, not to be indulged in. More like abstinence here, and all of our wants and desires are fulfilled there. Build temples, churches, and gluttonous hoop skirts here (for God's kingdom on earth), and have an equally glamorous mansion there. Glorious eventuality.

•••

I spoke to a friend of mine today to tell her how awesome she is. The Mother Teresa of cheerfulness. Mother of five, a perfect example of goodness, wholeness, decency, and happiness in adversity. I'm reserving for her a space in my honorary hall of sainthood. We spoke about our little girls. How sweet they are to be around. We talked about how her boys are all grown up. And how time goes by so fast. They are not chubby-cheeked toddlers anymore.

She reminded me how she is so glad that all things in her Christian world, will be rolled together as one. That all times, will be present simultaneously in heaven. Past, present, future. And, how she is so glad that she will have relations again with loved ones who have passed on. Young and old alike, each returning to an age that is their heavenly prime. Glorious eventuality.

She lives her life within the miracle of Christianity. What do I mean by that? I mean that I see her living a life that is within the boundaries of her hopes and dreams, which are tucked neatly within the boundaries of her God. Her satisfaction with her reality shows up on her radiant face, in her life.

This book isn't written for her. It is written for me, and for you. But, I bring my friend up to notice how happy she is with the thought that there exists a better life. The 'heavenly plan.' What you benevolently deserve, or that you deny yourself in this life will be settled out in the next. All those times you missed out on with your children, your lover, your friends, cha-ching, cha-ching, will come back to you in heavenly time travel. God will take care of my earth challenged omittances.

All of those wrongs you've righted, deeds you've forgiven, moments of pride you've stuffed down, blessings you've counted. 'Trust me.' They'll all pan out into one big fat heavenly pat on the back. The same day, you are given the golden key to your heavenly mansion.

Greedy bastards here, greedy bastards there, greedy bastards everywhere. Everyone pretending at goodness, or mercy, while their hands are in each other's pockets, groveling for control or acceptance, to pacify their existence. Earning heavenly credits for upgraded window treatments, and 90210 zip codes for that heaven's mansion.

•••

Years ago, in a great moment of silence, on a peculiar date, with blue-eyed Kris, I asked, in passing, to fill in the time (you get the picture),

"So, Kris, what do you think about life?"

Expecting the usual, "Hey, it's great." I instead found myself in a swimming, dizzy illusion of 'how many children she wanted', what her 'personal relationship with God' was like, and, what she felt deep inside about her 'relationship' with me. And before I could stall for time, she had blurted out the question,

"What do you think about life, Richard?"

God, it was our second date. What relationship with me? What children? What

'personal savior,' to get me out of this predicament?
I replied,

"Wherever you go in life, there you are."

I was new enough to that expression that it seemed novel to me. It worked. Or, at least, she seemed tempted back into silence by its absurdity at that moment. I drifted off into conversation about how physically committed to rock climbing and kayaking I was, and how I could never really get involved with those 'prissy' types, who wear lots of make-up, and paint their long delicate fingernails.
I was king of my verbiage. Gloating in my realist response to her ethereal question. I rolled over and belched in the fatness of the following silence. It was only then, that I noticed her long, delicately painted, China-doll fingernails, that she was fidgeting with in her lap.

Open mouth, insert ego. For obvious personal reasons, I decided to avoid kissing her goodnight on the porch that evening, and leaned forward to give her a hug instead. To which she responded in my ear,
"How did you know I love hugs more than kisses?"

I woke up the next morning, to find a finely decorated preserves jar on my front porch, filled with sweets. This was the old-fashioned type, with the metal-hinged glass lid that clamps down on one side. A piece of material, cross-stitched by hand, was mounted on the lid. It read,

"Wherever you go in life, there you are."

Home is where the heart is. Where your heart is, there your treasure will be, also. There are eight billion hearts on this planet, surrounded by their bodies, and their treasures. Everyone has their place. Theists, atheists, pacifists, nihilists, the list of 'ists,' goes on.
In the name of forgiveness, my friend Ben, has moved on to be a better man in spite of all my unforgiven anger towards his perpetrators. Ben found room for them. I'm finding room for my cynicism. And perhaps, in between, there is a grey area called reality. Saturated with the colors that we see in it. The momentary palette. The artist's eye. The camera's lens. Our physical communion with the stretched canvas recording our brush strokes.
I will have later, my best attempts at remembering now. This moment. Who I am. What I am doing. The colors that I am

feeling. The rewards that I am realizing now, are what I may count into stacks later. There is no later for this moment. A lesson that I'm learning, is to live without regrets. To live each moment, to its fullest, now. Whether I'm having, or having not, there is no later for this moment.

4

Garfunkelish epiphanies and fake throws.

I remember being in a remote area of the desert southwest, on another occasion, one particular equinox. We had planned the trip carefully. Big wood. Big fires. Good food. A mood-enhancing tea. An early morning hike into the wilderness of serpentine red canyons, towering sandstone walls, and undulating blonde clouds. A trickling stream. Dew-covered, head-high reeds, bathed our bodies as we walked through them. Bean-sized frogs. A white-tailed deer.

Rounding a bend in the streambed, we came upon an immense cavern, carved out of the overhanging canyon wall. The solid sandstone streambed and enveloping walls above echoed even the faintest sounds. The literal sound beauty of it all, hid from view, the strategically built, and precisely placed, millennia old, ceremonial ground. A remote desert sanctuary. Mud-caked kiva temples of an underground ancient order. Kept dry in winter by the high arching stone above.
Not spared by the ravages of erosion, the white-washed, slotted walls, and smoky ceiling of the most elegant kiva, were clearly

visible through its wall, damaged by seasons of flash floods. Handprints were memorialized in the worked plaster of their religion.

While the others had wandered off to inspect the other kivas, or to try out the acoustics of this grand place, I had remained behind to sit in silence at the grandest kiva. I wondered at the intentions of the builders. Their apparent awareness of symbolism. Binding with chords, the beams of the ceiling, into groups of two, on one side, and into groups of three, on the other. A draft-tunnel, built into the south wall of the kiva, fed the fire pit with fresh air from above. An upright deflector stone, prevented the fresh air from flowing right into the fire. I closed my eyes, and lay down on the earth to appreciate the stillness of this place.

No moving parts. Except the stars at night.

I could hear every word that the others spoke. As I listened to conversations about work, home, and city life, I began to wonder, why some in the group had bothered to travel hundreds of miles by car, and hours by foot, to get to this place. What were its secrets? What was it echoing?

I heard the pit-a-pat of my friend's fingers, tapping the earth six feet away from me. It sounded so distinct that I asked her, out of curiosity, if there was a slate of stone beneath her hand. Her response was to press her fingers deep into the earth, clear up to her wrist. I tapped on the soft earth where I was laying and found that it had the same acoustical resonance. Passing a beat back and forth through the belly of earth between us, we drummed out a mantra fitting for the moment.

Covered in dust, grinning from ear to ear, we recruited the others to come experience these strange acoustics. The nine of us sat in a circle and began coaxing a vibration out of the ground, in sync with the rhythm of the group. Raising up a dust that bathed our bodies in ritualistic primal energy, we continued the cadence, until the sound beauty of it all, came to its own single-noted end.

The silence was deafening. The engines of my mind had 'carpe diem'd,' and were seized with the moment. The meaning of life had been sedated, and replaced with reality. I reflect back now, and realize that I wasn't asking any questions, or solving any of life's riddles. I wasn't constipating my personal necessities into my want-filled mind.

It was like a Garfunkelish epiphany, minus the ten thousand people, the friend of darkness, and the neon light.

A moment later, the silence was broken by a thunder of chatter, as the group dispersed. My mind was instantly cast into unforgivable platitudes of how I would get back down to this area again, with this difference or that difference, maybe on a full moon solstice celebration or something. I was lost in the vision of how good this would be the next time I came back here again. I wanted so badly not to 'come down.' But the communal voice kept saying, 'We want to go back to camp.' The poppy field of my incredible journey, soon gave way to the clicking heals of their unanimity.

I've never returned to that place. The chubby face of its toddler-hood has given way to its puberty. Lives have changed. There hasn't been an eternal now. The scrolls of heaven never rolled-back together to give me my cinematic playback of oozing oneness. That moment, was. Wherever I had gone in life was there, at that moment. Preserved in a sweets jar, on the porch of reality.

That's why I don't believe in God. The small print in life is reality. NOW. NOW. NOW.

Believing in later may be hazardous to my health. Subtly abbreviating the reality of 'this,' for the hopeful eventuality of 'that.'

●●●

I hope I can get my whole story out, before I get soft on myself. Before I fall back into my own self-righteous pattern of 'forgiving and forgetting.' Allowing others to believe my lies. My lie of forgetting, my lie of forgiving. I know from my own experience, that I never forget. So, I never really forgive. This means I really am self-righteous, when I say, "I forgive you."

My story only comes out when I remember all of my misgivings, and tell the truths of all my 'turn the other cheek' lies. I was raised on the 'Thumper premise'. That is…

"If you can't say something nice…"

The little angel on my shoulder, keeps reminding me to write 'nice' things. Things that will be okay for everyone to read. To eat the easy fruit. But, the devil, if he is a devil, on my other shoulder, keeps saying,

"You won't die, write your true feelings…eat the forbidden fruit."

●●●

Back to the thought of gambling my life away with every trusted face card. Sounds so pathetic. That's why I am selective when I do it. I seem to trust very well, the situations, friends, and people, who I know very well. Regardless of what my mouth says, to appease itching ears.

For example, gambling with love in a steady relationship can be a low-risk investment. Like hippo love. A safe bet. Trust *can* work by default, when both lovers are being gambled on by each other. 'Trust,' in the form of an arrangement of controlled assumptions. None of this 'fools rush in' stuff.

In other words, each one is a casino boss. Let me see. That means that I get my ninety-seven percent back from what I gamble on my lover, plus, I keep three percent for the house from what my lover gambles on me. Each enjoying one hundred percent. No losers. All in all, a very excellent life. For everyone. Solid, man.

I believe, that it is the gambled commitments,

>...hope for things not seen,

>...rewards in a nebulous Heaven,

>...turning off the proverbial cheek,

>...the *losing* of oneself in the benevolent service of others,

that literally loses. Oneself. What a lousy investment. Into the lake. Into the bushes. The absolutely fake throw.

Love, hope, and willingness to believe in another person's benevolence. It's all the same thing. And we all do it to one degree or another. Learning the same lessons. The more I learn, the less I trust, the less I believe. Optimists at twenty. Pessimists at forty. Realists at fifty. Knowledge is king. And yet, I'll dive into the surf. Again, and again. Willing to entertain another coy forty-five.

What if the next time life flippantly tossed me a coy little forty-five, I flippantly tossed one back?

>"Yeah, no problem."

"That doesn't really matter."

"Oh, it was nothing."

"Believe me."

"It's O.K."

"Oh, and by the way, I forgive you."

It wouldn't exactly improve humanity, would it? And yet, it happens all the time. Souls lost in the service of wagging tails. Good dogs. Things not seen. Commitments not really as good as the breath that spoke them.

Hark! I hear my master calling.

"C'mon boy, good dog."

"Finish your story, people will care."

5

Overshadowing, is not a free-will event.

Hum. O.K. Let me go back to the Zodiac Killer story. That seems to be a memorable time period in my life. I met with my demon for the first time. Staring him in the belly. My first encounter with being absolutely alone. God wasn't everywhere. He was nowhere. Whatever goodness or rightness I might have acquired in my life, didn't amount to shit.
It was just me and my pounding heart.

•••

Born in the Fifties, and growing up in the Sixties, I found myself living in the emotionally turbulent Bay area. Concord, to be exact. Not exactly the Bay area. I was young enough to be bedazzled by all the far-out hippies in Golden Gate Park on Sunday afternoon drives. They'd be sleeping on the street corners. Sleeping in the median strips. Trafficking their homespuns. Smoking dope.

My older sisters admired the "sideburns" of groovy dudes. I never dared to ask them what sideburns were. I had to figure out that they weren't 'sunburned sides' on my own.

It had also become a frequent tradition to take our car down the insanely steep and curvy Lombard Street, in San Francisco. We'd drive past the salty, crabby smells of Fisherman's Warf, where navy ships seemed as tall as buildings. Sometimes, we were able to follow the trolley cars. But we would almost always eventually get lost in 'Hey Dashberry.' I thought the neighborhood was 'Dashberry,' and that the hippies were calling it, "Hey Dashberry."

The warm afterglow of Warm San Francisco Nights, hanging its furtive notes on hand-held transistor radios. And, I had convinced myself that I was sure to see one of the Beetles. Solid man. Here, where the deflowered intersection of *Haight-Ashbury,* broke water, and gave birth to long hair, bed rolls, flower power, miniskirts, afros, go-go boots, thirty-dollar guitars in store windows, bell bottoms, and enough beads and fringe to make it to the moon and back before Armstrong. If you went chasing rabbits in the sixties, you eventually ended up in Hey Dashberry.
"Just ask Alice."

I remember visiting Hearst's Castle. The family estate of the soon-to-be kidnapped Patricia Hearst. We were taken on school field trips to visit Chinatown, with all the smells of incense, smoke shops, and ginger-spiced candies. Storefront visions of cooked snails, live crabs, and meats hanging in the windows.

I remember driving past all the avenue whores in Oakland. Standing almost shoulder-to-shoulder. Touching the stove of a life so strange, so different from my own. Curiously odd. Driving by in the family Rambler. Windows rolled up tight. Eyes pressed up against the safety of the glass. Staring from the safety of my family. …But for the flaming swords and gaping abyss that separated my world from theirs.

I dreamed of growing up to be an Astronaut like my uncle Dean. I remember watching intently on our thirteen-inch black-and-white TV, while moonboots, filled with men, took their first steps on the moon. My uncle Dean was involved with the space program, from the early Apollo missions, and eventually to the Challenger missions.

On visits to our home, my brother and I would be given leaflets, and picture books of spacemen with their equipment. He would show us pictures of himself in weightlessness during spacewalk simulations. And, years later, he took my brother and me into the cockpit and crew quarters of an early space shuttle mock-up.

I remember watching the Blue Angel acrobatic jet pilots at air shows. Touring the Navy shipyards in the Bay, and being taken by my father to military expos that displayed military weaponry and attire.

I remember the smell, on the gear, on the cotton. A foreign musty odor, that brought to my mind images of the jungles in Viet Nam, where my cousin Reed was fighting. I remember seeing a battleship. Sensing the heartbeat of a war, I couldn't see. Much less understand. The mood was often somber, exciting, cool, and confusing at the same time. Marches in the streets. Stickin' it to the man.
Protesting battleships, wars, and the soldiers who fought in them. Celebrating space, rockets, and the men who flew in them.

Most memorable of all was the dreaded Zodiac Killer. Even more memorable than my friend Rod, throwing a hand shovel that stuck into the top of Craig Moody's head. More memorable than sinking on a homemade raft in the middle of Walnut Creek on a hot summer afternoon. More memorable than some hippies, being busted outside their van, and being searched for something apparently so small that the officers had to huddle around one open palm to poke at the booty of evidence.

There was even the little blonde freckled girl in third grade who showed me the mole on her prepubescent "place" down there beneath her dress and undies. There was no name for it back then. Alone in our illusionary 'house' made of tall golden California field grass behind the schoolyard. I showed her the mole on my right butt cheek. We noticed each other's differences, and it didn't seem to matter much.
We played several times after that. In my backyard, after school. One day, she gave me a nice large abalone shell. I don't remember what we did that day. Nothing particular that seemed to matter much. But I do remember my mom telling me that I wouldn't be playing with her anymore.
I found a safe place to bury my abalone shell under the shade tree outside my bedroom window.

I remember wondering why I was not to play with her anymore like my mother expected something to go wrong. Or, that maybe she thought something wrong had happened. Life wasn't about sex back then. Boys wore pants.

Girls wore dresses. We knew far too little to be guilty or innocent of our actions. In the absence of expectations and assumptions that come later with a libido and maturity, childhood friendships often remain a novelty in the human experience.

Speaking of boys wearing pants, I also met at that time a lifelong friend, Mark. I'm quite sure we are blood brothers, because we pricked our thumbs one day in his backyard, and watched until a cherry of blood formed, and then we pressed them together.

Well, one day, I saw his older sister Kathy wearing jeans when she came home. Girls never wore jeans. She was a free spirit, like my older sister. Not a churchgoer. The jeans even opened in the front. So, in private, I had to ask Mark if his sister had a penis. I found out that Mark knew more about those things than I did. From that day on, I understood that all girls, whether wearing dresses or pants, look just like my third-grade friend did when we showed our vulnerability to each other.

On hot summer days, Mark and I would do chores to earn a swim in the only backyard pool in our neighborhood. Taking a cool dip one day, we found that we could get the small body of water to move clockwise slowly, if we would just move along the edges of the pool like monkeys in the water. Churning the mill, like Amlodhi's Quern, we found that in our search for making a whirlpool, we had rather succeeded in removing the skin off of all our toes. The stinging and burning of our raw sores that followed, stuck to our socks and made walking to school torture for the next week. Later in life, I would find that the search for oneness and love, may be much like that search for 'querning' a whirlpool. Successful only in removing the skin off of one's searching soles.

Near the schoolyard, we also discovered a corrugated steel drainage culvert, about three-feet high, and perhaps fifty-yards long. This we knew, ran all the way to the Walnut Creek, sticking-out like a cigar where it ended, high over the creek below. As kids will do, we double-dog dared each other, and made the long crawl through the stinking mud and yuck and spiders to reach the view below. The crawl back was always the scariest part, as the "monsters in the abyss," seemed to mock our gift of roses, and the circle of light seemed so infinitesimally small and impossible to reach.

When we reached the safety of daylight again, our hunger would find satiety in baking a snack of toast at Mark's house. White Wonder bread. Toasted in the oven. And Mark always made sure to put four large slices of butter on each piece. Details that I never experienced at my home. And if Wonder bread was not around, he would grab two spoons from the kitchen, and a whole quart of ice cream from the freezer in his garage, and we would climb up into the rafters above, and eat the whole thing.

I remember being pulled on metal-wheeled roller skates behind Mark's banana seat bike, except past Deedee's house. She, for some unknown reason, had been dubbed the name Deedee Underarm. It was the ultimate insult to call someone a Deedee Underarm.

And speaking of insult, I remember peeing my pants in elementary school when the principal, insane with anger, demanded I get down from the basketball hoop where I was sitting to have a better view of the track races.

Then there was the time I remember being in our upstairs bathroom. I was with a girl who must have been an older babysitter or something. She was taller and more aware of whatever it was that she wanted. I remember standing with my back up against the bathroom wall, and she was in front facing me. Both of us were naked. She kept asking me to stick my penis, 'right here.' I didn't know what 'right here' meant. So, I kept touching my penis, 'right here.' I wasn't doing something the right way. She seemed annoyed.

To this day, I still question how we even ended up together alone in that bathroom of a four-bedroom home that I shared with five siblings and my parents.

For now, I mean back then, my thoughts were more driven by the usual childhood events. Playing neighborhood games. One in particular, being the Zodiac Killer game, which brings me back to the most memorable thing, the Zodiac Killer.
We had a game much like hide and seek, except we called whoever was 'IT,' the Zodiac Killer. Which was really the nickname of a serial killer who was going around killing people in the Bay area near my home. We didn't know what Zodiac meant except that our night-games that summer would be abbreviated by a nightly enforced curfew. Perhaps that's what made the game more mysterious. I didn't like being alone and hiding. He could be out there spying on us.

●●●

However 'aware' I was of the reality of our little game, I was very unaware of reality. Perhaps being raised on the 'milk and honey' of the bible, I was naïve to the nonbenevolent intentions of strangers in my perfect world. At least, what I know about the day it happened is that, for some reason, I allowed myself to trust a total stranger. Of course, a stranger in need.

Mark and I were playing baseball on his street with some friends. A car pulled up slowly. The man driving seemed lost. He slowed to a stop and was inaudibly asking a question. I went over to help him. He wanted to know where the shortcut was that cut through the large field behind the elementary school to the other side of the neighborhood. The one that bypassed the longer route around the lumberyard.

I knew right where it was. Mark and I played there often. A large pond would often gather in the middle of the field when the drenching winter rains came. I explained in detail how he needed to drive around the block to the small cul-de-sac at the back of the school field. There would be a dirt road with an iron gate.

He said he had been there, but that he couldn't find the dirt road.

Next, he asked if I would get in his car to show him the way. I hesitated. He then asked if I would help him by riding my bicycle around the block to show him where it was. I must have considered his proposal to be a safe one, like a deceptive coy forty-five. Perhaps I was excited by the prospect of being a good Samaritan, and helping someone. Or, of being able to speed around the block on my bike. Or, perhaps I just couldn't say NO. So, I pedaled around the block. The man in the car followed right behind me. I took him right to the cul-de-sac. Right to the dirt road. Right to the gate.
God, I even wanted to open the gate for him.

I remember an odd and vulnerable feeling as I got off my bike to check the lock. Out of the corner of my eye, I noticed he had gotten out of his car. I felt everything around me all of a sudden seem unfamiliar, like tunnel vision. I realized, much too late, the precarious nature of my situation. A gut feeling. A foreboding. The gate was locked. I didn't want to be there alone with that man. In the split second, it took me to realize all these things, he had quickly approached me at the gate.

I turned and picked up my bike to leave, but he grabbed me by the arm, demanding that I leave my bike where it was. Nearly lifting me off my feet, he forced me over to a nearby jog in the wooden fencing at the back of the school field. It was somewhat protected by trees that ran along a ditch. My mind was reeling with the impending finality of my desperate seclusion. I remember feeling a sickening wrongness, a fear that this man was overwhelmed by his power over me. My legs wouldn't support me as he pushed me up against the fence. My frantic ramblings to talk my way out of it dribbled out of my mouth. Mocking me with their futility. The smell of cheap men's cologne was nauseating. I was choking on my life. Trying to keep it swallowed. But he was humping it out of me.

So perhaps I wasn't too young after all for the sixties. Perhaps, as my friend Shawn told me after reading some of my manuscript, I'm just using my stories as mental images to keep you, my readers, safely distanced from the truth. He says I need to finish my story. Come out of my closet. But I can't. My closet is nailed up against a fence. At the end of a dirt road. By the schoolyard. Somewhere between the sweaty, suffocating sweater and my silent screams for Jesus. The closet is

empty, and next to it is a bloody robe and a sign that reads, "He is risen."
I was only seven or eight. Frightened. Thinking that I might die. Making up lies like "My mom is going to be mad if I'm not home for dinner." I knew that I might not *ever* be going home for dinner. I felt his weight press hard against me.

Things happened that I was too young to understand. But hey! After all, this was the sixties, and perhaps he knew more about overshadowing and free love than I needed to know in my lifetime. You figure out the rest. And perhaps I, like Rob in the desert, was sexually "outed" before my time, and I have enough anger hidden under years of conditioning to dent a few 'heirloom' silver trays and Chevy vans myself.

The bottle did say, "Drink Me." I was definitely NOT Mickey with the wizard's hat on. I was screaming for the wizard to help me. Brooms were multiplying, marching towards me, with much too much water.
I was soon to be baptized as a Mormon and perhaps needed to learn by experience the principles of 'love' and 'overshadowing' that I would later learn as patriarchal Christianity and evangelized bullying in the name of 'covenant' peoples.' The irrational behavior

that can overtake someone overwhelmed by their libido, is closely resembled by the irrational behavior of those overwhelmed by their belief process.

●●●

See, I'm diffusing again. Using cynicism to delay my story from you. But you see, my story is stuck somewhere between my right-hand piece of mushroom and my left-hand piece of mushroom, with a pre-transformed, hookah-sucking caterpillar sitting on a toadstool before me asking, "Who are you?" So, if you are very patient, somewhere between the beginning and end of this book, I will tell you things like why I was sleeping with a loaded gun outside my bedroom door, why I pondered burying Rob in the desert, and why we were all naked in the first place. Just follow the rabbit. The one in my story, with the pocket watch, who has time all mixed up front ways and back ways. Maybe he, too, has a fence to mend, a story to tell, and a giant or two pressing it out of him.

God! A thought just came to me during that last sentence. Maybe if I follow the rabbit, he might lead me back into that empty closet of mine, and I might come out the other side playing baseball with my friends, reciting perfect English, seven years old, on time for dinner, on the other side of the closet from Mickey, Alice and endless streams of metaphor.

My faithful friend, the rabbit, keeps telling me to write. To tell you what I'm feeling right now. This was my first experience of being absolutely alone. Forsaken by all my gods. My faith couldn't save me. I was left with a fig leaf of inevitability, which became my first step toward later in life becoming a humanist, and to a feeling, that there is no 'great cause,' or 'common good,' or 'savior' outside of my own being. I felt the utter smallness of my insignificance. The absoluteness of unnatural selection.

What little I knew about life was flashing before my eyes. My demons. My fears. A sickening confusion of what I knew about boys and girls being hurled at me with his suffocating sexual frenzy. I was feeling death. Beyond my own ability to determine fate. A creaking fence, the only sound of my requiem.

●●●

I remember, as a child, playing in a neighborhood Carrom tournament. A game much like pool, but small enough to fit in my upstairs bedroom. The final contenders for the summer break championship were my friend and I. Turn for turn, we reached the moment where I had had one final easy shot to take the game. James would lose. Winning the game would be less glorious for me than what happened on my next move. I calculated just how hard I would need to hit my cue piece so that my final shot would end up just short of the pocket. James' next turn won the game and the tournament. I was secretly elated for him. Not that he won, really, so much as that he didn't have to lose.

●●●

Out of nowhere, a kid I knew from school darted by on his bike. I wanted to scream, but only silence came out. My god, I thought. Come back. Come back. Perhaps the 'Zodiac' was listening to my thoughts. Or, perhaps I really was screaming. After what seemed like an eternity, my glimmer of hope happened. He stopped what he was doing and walked me back over to his car.

I remember thinking that I would not see my bike again. You may think that trivial. But ownership of anything, attachment to anything, connection to *anything* gave me hope, and feeling that I wouldn't see my bike again felt like this was the end for me. I stammered something about my bike. I can't remember what I said or did to keep him from putting me into his car. At some point, the kid from school came pedaling back past us again. This time, he stared at us for a long time. The man let go of my arm, quickly got into his car, and left me standing there. Alone.

Some may call that the 'hand' of a god, or a 'miracle', or karmic recompense for my precisely calculated Carrom shot. What I know is that it happened, and that I was left alone to make sense of it all.

•••

It took me an hour to make the five-minute ride back around the block. I didn't know who to tell, or what to tell, or what the hell happened. How do I answer, "What did he do?" at seven years old? I didn't understand what happened myself, let alone fluidly remembering the details. While he was pounding my groin with his crotch, I was babbling nonsense. So, instead of going straight home, I went back to Mark's house. To the baseball game.

I think Mark sensed something was wrong and eventually encouraged me to go home. I don't remember what I told or how I told my parents. I do remember that my dad had me get into the car and we went driving around Concord looking for the stranger's car. I don't know what would have happened if we had found it. We never did.

I often had nightmares of his car approaching me on the street again. I still occasionally smell his same pungent cologne on someone when I'm in a crowd of people.

•••

The following year I got baptized a Mormon. I supposed that the feeling dirty, and the feeling guilty feelings would be washed away. That I would be as white as snow. But it was rather uneventful. I found that not talking about it worked better than trying to wash it away.

Three years later, we moved from Concord. Partly to get my two older sisters away from the hippies that had become the center of the adolescent world in northern California. Two years after that, my oldest sister just disappeared. For almost a year. That was about the time of the highly publicized kidnapping of Patty Hearst. The search was on for my sister, and my search was on for a new identity.

●●●

Life is time. Time is life. And time is carried on watch fobs by synapses in my brain that are busily hopping along chanting, "I'm late, I'm late" for my next appointment with life. And just like that, I am compelled to get to my next idea, find my next interest, and trust my next forty-five.

If you feel that I'm rambling, skip ahead a few pages; you won't miss a thing. "Trust me."

6

Ode to Theseus.

Gaston was the first real friend that I met after my family had moved away from the Bay area. I found myself surrounded by …

Sorry, I am back now.

Gaston was also considered an outsider to our neighborhood. He lived down the street over by the bike trails in a completely different neighborhood. So, to reach his home from the school yard, he would have to run the gauntlet of boys who ran the neighborhood at the exit from the school yard. He was six inches shorter than most of the boys in middle-school. He was considered an outsider for something as silly as that. For being from a different neighborhood and being a little shorter. Well, okay, and also for being like a 'David' when the tensions boiled over into all-out apple and apricot wars between the 'kingdoms.' Skilled as he was with precisely aimed fruit, Gaston learned perhaps, during these experiences, that his words worked better than a slingshot.

From a very young age, Gaston was gifted with a photographic memory and the ability to dress his tongue in the mini-skirt and high-heels of sarcasm and cynicism. Like a court jester, he let-fly stones that would certainly bring to the knee most, but for their delight and titillation in Gaston's skillful gift with his word-stones. Often being both angered and humored, by the agility with which he colored and teased the nectar out of his eloquent, cynical, humorous reenactments of situations, people, and events. The way Gaston did it was, at the same time, offensive and endearing. The way many other kids did it, just made them look like they had eaten too much sugar, or that they were on drugs, or both.

Something almost magical happened around Gaston. He was like a court priest, a court magician, and a court jester, steeped in a tea of nightshade and wormwood, and washed down with the milky green 'devil's potion.' Every hour was like the mental equivalent of 'the green hour' with Gaston. He was the kid who was the imitation of an Evil Knievel when we raced off to the bike trails, and like a Jack Nicholson in The Shining, when he bored too easily of our ninth-grade obligatory typing classes, and finally, like an Albert Einstein when it came to remembering word for word the exact laws of expansion that are challenged by filling a small pipe with grains of gun powder and then screwing a steel cap on both ends. The laws of expansion were definitely under-stated that time though, and there was nothing left of that brick mailbox.

Gaston never hesitated when given the opportunity to freak with people. Including the time that we were driving together with some friends, and, without notice, from the back seat, Gaston reached his hands around the face of the one driving and pulled his head back into the headrest. Like his version of water-boarding, while the driver did their best to keep their hands on the steering wheel. I laughed good at that one. I wasn't the one driving. We barely avoided catastrophe. Tossing caution to the wind, before we even adequately understood wisdom. Life in those days, pre-helmet, pre-sea-belt use, pre anti-skid breaks, did seem 'easy baby,' as was then aptly being sung by the band, ZZ Top.

One day, we were on an 'epic of Gilgamesh' in the field behind Gaston's house. I must have been fourteen or so. Always keen to have the latest and coolest things, he had just purchased a new compound bow and was eager to show it to all of us. Carefully removing each of the aluminum-shaft, steel-tipped arrows from the packaging, Gaston then proceeded to carefully load one in the bow and pull back the string. With a zing, the arrow disappeared out of sight above us. The 'wows,' the 'oohs,' and the 'aahs,' were instantly silenced as we all looked at Gaston. Looking back at us, with the usual glimmer in his eye, he shrugged his shoulders as if to say, "Well….." We scattered in all directions at once. The one laughing the most was Gaston, as he watched most of us scramble into the bushes or for cover under his back porch.

Not long after we had moved from the Bay area, my grades fell to C's and D's. Too many unlucky coincidences had happened at early stages in my life, I guess. A lack of confidence can do that. I became familiar with the phrase 'who gets Richard.' Familiar, like Gaston, with being smaller, and an outsider. Familiar with often being picked last. Unfamiliar with bullies and group mentality. Either football and basketball sucked, or I sucked at both. The latter was mostly true.

Here, in my new home, I found my first exposure to clans, to exclusion, and to little fat kids, too young for puberty, telling me to 'go home', of course from under the shadow of the neighborhood-bully's watchful eye.

One school year, I was bullied back into my yard for six months by the neighborhood clan. Boys who were sons of priests, sons of good parents, Sunday-go-to-meet'n boys. Mouths full of brownie points earned in Sunday school, only to spit the walnuts out at me on the walk home from church. I would often hop my back fence and sneak through the schoolyard to make friends in other neighborhoods.

My life began to change only as I was finishing Junior High in the mid-seventies. It was at this time that a happy accident, my *objet trouvé*, occurred while on a camping trip with my family in Jackson Hole, Wyoming. I loved these summer trips. I could walk off on my own, enjoy fishing, and mostly reminisce about my childhood visits to Lake Tahoe or Mount Shasta.

Well, one day, I was not particularly lucky at fishing. My father asked if I would be interested in signing up for a rock climbing class with him and my older brother. The rock-climbing classes were exhilarating. It seemed that I had finally found something that interested me, where winning did not compromise, or put others beneath me to do so. And my smaller size didn't matter. It was here that I found myself excelling at something. Challenging myself. Being better than myself, and not feeling guilty afterwards. It felt like peaking behind the curtain. Like catching the magician at his trick. Like I could at once go out and compete with myself, and even win.

For Christmas that year, my father gave me my first twisted Goldline climbing rope. With snow still, on the ground, I remember riding on my three-speed motorcycle down to Gaston's house with my new rope over my shoulder to show him my new distraction. Within moments, we were climbing up the large oak tree outside his bedroom window, searching for the summit. We each had on a make-shift harness that we had tied out of lengths of nylon webbing. Securing the rope to one of the highest branches, we set up a rappel, lowering the rope like our ode to Theseus. We each then shared the single carabiner that I owned, to wildly descend the single strand of rope. Somehow, we avoided killing ourselves.

We found a way to rock climb almost every free day after that. Back in those days, we would usually thumb rides to our favorite climbing spots. Climbing gear was a relative oddity and rather expensive. We could make about three dollars per driveway shoveling snow. That was the cost of a single carabiner, or of a single wired stopper. We prayed for snowstorms. One wired stopper at a time, one carabiner at a time, we began to accumulate our gear. Later that Spring, we started charging three dollars per hour for doing yardwork, and our gear began to accumulate. Twist by twist and braid by braid, the ginger trestles of my muse began to cast their roses into my abyss.

In 1975, after ninth-grade graduation, I returned with my father and my brother to Wyoming. This time we had done more research, and we paid a mountaineering instructor to guide us up the Grand Teton together. I still keep in my library a piece of granite that my father carried down from off of the summit. He had it engraved with all of our names.

Our fascination with rock climbing included our intention to maintain the purity of what was happening in Yosemite Valley and the climbing world. This meant vigilantly protecting our rock crags from visiting climbers who might use gym chalk on their hands that would then leave nasty chalk marks all over the rock faces after they left our canyons. We would even sometimes carry a broken-off toothbrush to clean away any unsightly chalk left by non-purist climbers.

Something rare had happened in Yosemite Park, California, that season. Half-Dome had been ascended by a team of climbers using the new fad of 'free climbing.' In just thirty-two hours, Art Higbee and his partner Jim Erickson had scaled the entire North Face, a feat that previously required up to five full days. All but one of the twenty-three rope pitches had been done with no aid. This meant that no pitons were hammered into cracks. No bolts were drilled into rock faces, and all the ascent gear had to be removable and not violate the rock in any way. This meant that climbing all of the twenty-three pitches had been done using only wired nuts and stoppers, like the ones that Gaston and I were collecting. These could be placed into the irregularities in cracks, and then easily maneuvered back out when retrieved.

It would be ten more years before the development of spring-loaded camming devices called 'Friends', or any similar type of expandable and removable climbing gear that has been in common use since the eighties. Using only these small removable 'nuts', the team had placed and then retrieved them hundreds of times into the cracks of

Half Dome's North Face, leaving no evidence or damage behind. They had used no aid, nothing but sheer human skill, except for aid *etriers* for a few feet on the twenty-second pitch. This was the seventies. Most rock climbers were still climbing in Vibram-soled leather hiking boots. Art and his partner, Erick, were wearing what I would later find out to be 'EB's,' an absolutely momentous improvement in rock climbing. I imagined this shoe being comparable only to the invention of the toe-box dance shoe for ballerinas. And it was not long before I owned my first pair.

I had carefully removed the pages of this climbing story from a National Geographic during my sophomore year, and they were now pasted on my bedroom walls. My new muse, 'free climbing.' I studied the articles often. Something about the competition being within one's own self inspired me. I dreamed about becoming the best at it.
We climbed 'to never fall.'

The uncertainty that accompanied the use of only temporary and retrievable climbing gear meant that one was never certain of the temporary placements as one ascended. This meant that falling was really not an option. In many ways, it was like climbing free without

ropes. Today, with most climbs protected by a string of bolts that have been drilled into the rock face, bolts that each hold thousands of pounds, a climber is pretty much bush-league if an ascent does not include many lead-falls on that dependable equipment.
Climbing rather, 'until one falls.'

My confidence improved, as did my grades, which trended more towards B's and A's. One year later, I was standing again on top of the Grand Teton, this time with Gaston on our first ascent of that mountain together. And, when we graduated from high school two years after that, we took a road trip to North-Eastern Wyoming and climbed the compelling and, at that time, relatively unknown Devils Tower monument.

I did not write this book for Gaston either. He never seemed to have a need to choke gods. Never seemed to hold himself back, or to give- in to coy forty-fives, or to give to one's neighbor, before giving to oneself. He constantly bent the rules of conformity, mocking them with his jest. He could mock the humor out of most situations. Except for this once. It was Winter formal. We had just dropped off our dates for the evening. He had managed to borrow his father's Cadillac for the evening. On the way home, sailing through one corner at twice the normal speed, we bottomed-out the Cadillac while passing through a gutter, and sent it flying towards a house, stopped only by a retaining wall, and a four-foot drop that left the car teetering into the owners front yard.

When Gaston's father arrived to see the damage, Gaston immediately went into damage control with a story that would have rivaled Samson's. "…The icy road." "…The deep gutter." "…The old tires." Gaston's father, perhaps like most people, humored by Gaston's agile ability with words, finally turned to him and said, "You can tell people it was the ice, or the gutter, or the tires, …but between you and me you know that's bullshit." You can't kid a kidder. Gaston rarely ever used coy forty-fives. And his father was not the type to ever follow them.

Apologies are for non-deliberate people. Gaston was confident and deliberate in a big brother sort of way. Rarely excusing a choice, or a deliberate action, with meaningless drivel. Begging forgiveness is lost on the deliberate, and on the confident. Except for this one time. After there had been a particularly long abbreviation to our visits, and, long after I had met with the jubilation of vegetation at the Belvedere. Gaston showed up on my front porch one day. He simply said, "I'm sorry, brother." Twenty years later, I still feel that moment in my chest. It remains to me still as my most valued and genuine I'm 'sorry.' Roughhewn. Not polished. Not faceted to dazzle with words. An outstretched hand, presenting a palm, full of vulnerability.

Sorry, is hiding underneath the gluttonous fat hoop skirt of an apology, which is hiding underneath the gluttonous fat hoop skirt of asking for forgiveness, which is standing in front of being highly ingenuous, which is standing in front of being highly deliberate, which is surrounded by…

Sorry, I just got back again.

7

Sisyphus meets Don Quixote.

The first time I ever fought someone was in fifth grade. It was after school one day, in the schoolyard. I was not the best at marbles, but I could get by. Marbles were boss. Everybody played them at recess. Littlies. Half-pints. Biggies. Boulders. Steelies, from Dad's tool drawer. Resins, from Mom's homemade grape clusters she made at a church social. Marbles were more important than girls. Or perhaps I was less important to girls. Girls rarely played. They mostly watched.

The game was played by "setting-up" a marble. This was done by first marking a "shooters" line in the grass. At this line, boys would pull littlies out of their pockets, kneel, and shoot at whatever had been "set-up." The person setting-up would sit on the ground with their legs apart, position a marble in front of them and yell, "setting-up..." whatever they had positioned in front of them. All the littlies that missed were keepers. The set-up marble was turned over to the boy who had shot and hit it. As we ran outside for recess, shouts could be heard, "setting-up a biggie," "hit one get three," and so on.

Chris was the best. He would come to school with just a few marbles and leave for home with both of his pockets stuffed. Boys learned to keep their set-ups away from Chris. He would shoot and hit on the first shot. Not a good gamble. Unless you were Chris, I, as I said, could get by. I would come with a pocketful of marbles and leave with less than a pocketful unless I had been able, during the last class period, to finish one of my moving picture books that I would draw in sequence at the bottom of small notepads. These I would trade for marbles. On a good day, I, too, would go home with a pocketful of marbles.

On the day it happened, I was low on marbles. I had no picture books to trade. My only hope was to find a tuft of grass to position my set-up behind so most shooters would miss. It worked. That is until Chris walked over to my set-up, kneeling at the shooters' line; he shot one, two, three, and kept missing. With each miss, he got angrier. Finally, he stood, walked over to my set-up, and grabbed a handful of the keepers from between my legs.

What ensued became a blur. Now, I had seen my friend Steve, fist fight Ricky in the church field after school. He beat him in the face till Ricky could not stand on his own, but had to be held up by his 'buddies' for the second and third rounds. His knees buckling under the weight of his nearly unconscious body. The crowd seemed bloodthirsty. Anxiously cheering on Ricky and Steve, to keep the fight going.

I would later in life recall the same sickening feeling I felt inside that day. At fifteen years old. Deer hunting. I remember the shot and near lifeless animal lying in the creek into which it had fallen. I had watched the deer frantically trying to escape the canyon on the ledges above and finally lose its footing after being shot in the jaw. The fall over the ledges had mangled its body. The 'absolute control' of the hunters had given little consideration to the fact that the deer would fall sixty feet, over two ledges, before hitting the ground as useless inedible meat. Gasping for air through its flapping jaw, it was an unequal match for the 'skill' and 'marksmanship' of the hunter who, at point blank, determined the last glimmer in its beautiful doe eyes. I would decide then and there to never hunt again. Ever.

It's difficult to put a finger on just exactly what caused me to beat Chris that day. Perhaps watching that guy Ricky lose that fight? Losing to the 'Zodiac?' Peeing my pants in front of my principal? Having something stolen from between my spread legs again? The bread of my life slithered down my throat and cast itself about in my flesh. I went straight for Chris's throat. We fell to the ground, and I choked him till he couldn't breathe. He bit clear through the skin on my knuckle. He would writhe. I would choke harder. I knew that one thing was 'absolutely' certain.

… I was not letting go until he gave up.

Chris said, "Give" that day, clear enough to mean he was finished. I had no friends to cheer me on. No advantage of size. No fist-fighting practice. In fact, the crowd seemed somewhat disappointed that only a few punches were thrown, as if my fighting style wasn't good enough for them. God, I nearly killed him. I was angry as hell. And I'm not a violent person. Including the time that I smashed Tom to the ground with that gallon jug of water. But somehow, I had acted before my fee-fi-fo-fum god-fearing mind could get in my way with benevolence or forgiveness. Tossing myself a crushed bone,

I had awakened my self-respect and made-off with the golden goose that the *giant* concept of God often obscures from the natural instinct township of my psyche.

●●●

How many cultures, peoples, and races have been sold out and lobotomized by belief in gods? How many golden geese have been stuffed into fat calves as sacrifices or tithings to gods who promise to fight someone's battles in exchange for contrition and humility? Save the whales? The rainforest? That's like wiping my ass to change my diet. And doing it with nice, soft, scented, 2-ply, quilted toilet paper. Unrecycled, of course.

Don't get me wrong. I'm not indifferent to the plight of our diminishing species of aquatic friends and ozonating fauna. But the truth is, garbage in, garbage out. Garbage in the form of absolute superiority has given humankind a desensitized view of how very delicate biological life's place is on this planet. No matter how red we paint the roses, the whales and rainforests keep dying.

Superiority has become a weed. A pest. A mad-adder. Choking the life out of the very trees of life. Biting their heels with our incessant, top-of-the-food-chain, 'off with their heads' mentality. Move over natural world; superiority is coming through chaining down your forests to rape them and make room for its drug-sedated, teat-bloated cows and cash-mongering coffee fields. …Or is it killing fields?

How about the brotherhood of man climbing up the beanstalk to reclaim our natural instinct and tribal music from our 'gods in heaven.' Storm the Bastille of our belief systems. Free humanity's imprisoned minds from the notion that something or somebody will make everything all better for us. Stretch a condom over the crony capitalistic head of man-unkind. Man gone berserk. Man betraying his brothers and sisters for thirty pieces of silver disguised as world welfare, state medicine, social security, national security, or heaven's purity. Choke the greedy bastard in us all until absolute senselessness says 'give' to reason and responsibility. Save mankind from the *giant* multi-national gods we've created. Cut the umbilical beanstalk that keeps mediocrity enslaved to nobility.

You want to save the whales? Choke the society that senselessly abuses their lives. Save the rainforest? How about just choke our beef eating and need for lumber. Be saved from sin? Choke your god. Wring his gluttonous neck until you get all your marbles back along with your common sense, good reasoning, and self-worth.

●●●

In the end of the Seventies, I found myself taking a sabbatical from reaching new summits. …Not by choice, but in the end, it was essential to my process of putting the jigsaw puzzle of my life together like one of those lost pieces that are found under the rug or in the vacuum, long after you have put the puzzle away.

I was living at 203 Knickerbocker Avenue, in Brooklyn, near Williamsburg, where I had been assigned to 'take census' in the 'Norths' and the 'Souths.' I loved walking in the older backstreets and picking pieces of history out of the cracks in the cobblestones. I loved following the smell of fresh bread and Challah at Sander's bakery near the Williamsburg Bridge. Or perhaps I was lucky enough to get invited to dinner at my friend's house in Bushwick, where his sweet Puerto Rican mother made the best *tostones y habichuelas* ever.

When I tired of burning my attempts at tostones, I could always just pop downstairs to Joe and Mary's Pizzeria next door to have Brooklyn's best meatball sandwich, with its light hint of fennel, a favorite of the Sicilian elite who gathered there often.

This particular block, between Jefferson and Troutman, had yet to earn its reputation as 'The Well,' and as New Yorks 'toughest drug den.' This coveted title was, in the seventies, still in the glorious hands of 'Hell's Kitchen' in the city's lower west side. Its jeweled crown was laden with drugs, prostitutes, needles and homicides.

But the reputation of this block, my block, as the crowned jewel in New York of homicides and drugs, would happen a decade later in the early nineties, long after the overnight years of fame, which were to follow the events of me leaving my apartment on that day, Wednesday, July twelfth.

My apartment had no air conditioning, which also meant it had no laundry. I had lugged my cleaning up to a laundry mat on Troutman two blocks away. After spending a couple of hours, I made my way back down to Knickerbocker with my folded laundry over my shoulder in my bag. The street ahead was filled with people, and more were coming. Blue wooden police barricades failed at keeping the mob from pressing into the street, making it impossible for me to walk just halfway down the block back to my apartment.

There was an ambulance in front of my building. My immediate thought was for my landlord, who was a dear old lady from Seoul, Korea. But with all the nearly hundred locals who had gathered from up and down the street, I felt certain that this did not concern her. As I stepped further into the crowd, I could hear whispers. "The mob..." " Haven't come out..." "The police are still…"

Any loud noises reminded the crowd of the recent gunshots, and most were visibly still jumpy. After what seemed like hours in the sweltering July humidity, what appeared like first one, then two, then three body bags were carried out of the front door of Joe and Mary's, into the waiting ambulances. Carmine Galante, the godfather of the Bonanno crime family in New York, along with two of his men, had been gunned down. The scene was a chaos of onlookers. The street was kept closed to manage the crowds. And the next few hours seemed like a street-wake, as I drifted from conversation to conversation of how 'this' or 'that' had certainly gone down.

Later that evening, my curiosity was sated, as I gazed from my third-floor balcony down onto the private patio behind the pizzeria, where Carmine had last been famously photographed with his usual cigar still hanging limply from his now quiet lips. The stains on the cement, which would take a winter to fade to a pale brown, were now quite crimson still in the flat light of that late summer evening between the buildings.

As I clipped out news articles over the next few days, only then did I realize just where I was living, and on just what street, with just what unresolved heat, of just which conversations. With just whom, over the last few weeks, had I been sharing shoulders, over bowls of limp Bolognese?

Later that hot evening, when the humidity seemed to rise back out of the pavement, and children were back to making street fountains out of fire hydrants, a deafening explosion rocked the stadium at Comisky Park. White Sox fans who attended the double-header that night, were joined by more than twenty thousand angry music fans wearing 'disco sucks' T-shirts and each bringing their collection of hated disco records. The records overflowed the huge burn-bin that had been prepared for a large demonstration in the center of the field after the first game. The massive explosion had decimated the bin of records and had damaged the field. A large riot followed. The second game was cancelled. And disco, too, suffered its death wound that night. The Roseland, Studio 54, and many other similar establishments becoming mausoleums to absurdity, and to the freedom of expression that had once been nailed like an emancipation to their front doors. Another decade would go by before expressions would once again be freed, only to collide again with phobias and isms that would again press the sensibility out of our human dilemma. The absurdity of Sisyphus, indifferently raising up the crucified Quixote, as if he were a huge boulder, on the cross-like wings of the windmill. Again. And again. And yet again.

Strange days those were, as the seventies came to a close, in New York, where John, unknowingly, still had just five months remaining to 'imagine all the people.' Perhaps he actually 'knew,' on some level, why some 'were saying goodbye,' while he was 'saying hello." And the world bid him his last goodbye on Seventy-Second street that winter.

•••

I had planned one Summer to meet some friends for a week at the lake. My friends had arranged for the hotel and had arrived early on the first day. Earlier that day, they had also decided to take ecstasy. In the early nineties, it was the newest novelty available that delivered 'oneness' and 'free love' in a cute little capsule.

I arrived at one o'clock in the morning. They were coming down. Adam in God's wife's arms, and God in the Virgin Mary's' arms. Love and oneness oozing all over the place. They wanted me to join them as if it would go on forever. The Being of Light had already told them to go back and get the others. In other words, they were coming down. Recruiting is the proper name for it. I got to do that after I had made it to my third-level transformational training retreat.

•••

But what about the consideration? I just wanted to consider lilies, not recruit. The lilies… they toil not, neither do they sow. As in nada. They do nothing but sit in fields. They don't sow. They don't toil. And they get arrayed anyway. Like the kid who cries and moans for *everything*, and gets everything. Only the lilies don't even complain. Not even a little. They just toil not, and lay in the sun. And when they get tired of getting arrayed and sitting in the sun, they just sit there and get arrayed anyway. And don't sow, and get arrayed. And don't toil and get arrayed. And drink, and lie, and grow.

But free love, oneness, transformation, and mystical experiences, all come down. Always preceded by the urge to get others to join the party. "Turn on, tune in, drop out." Join your hands together. Love one another. The urge to be one. …But that's not really how it goes.

As soon as Eve got Adam to eat the 'fruit' of transformation, they got kicked out of the garden in Eden. The characters will always get kicked out of their symbolic garden in Eden and will have to make it on their own. In other words, they will 'come down.' The trip doesn't last forever. And there are bills to pay, planes to catch and videos to rewind in the morning.

The good part is that it will be coming again soon to a theatre near you. And, for the price of a ticket, or the proper obedience, you can fool your senses into thinking and feeling like you are 'there' again. And you will. Oh yeah, sing it with Mr. Costello,

"My aim is true."

Yeah, and if I hear one more new-age version of,

…"And then I found myself moving up this tunnel of white light."

"…I saw this pure white being." (oops).

"…this being of pure white light."…

(Of course, clothed with flowing robes from BCE, complete with sandals, open chest, fair skin, blue eyes and flowing hair)…

"And, he said to me that I must go back and tell the others,"

… I'll scream 'book sales!' 'Hugged by the light.' 'Visited by the light.' 'Embraced in the light.' 'Blinded by the light.' Yes, blinded by the light. Oneness, love, transformation, and mysticism, are all beautiful and wonderful while they are up, high, and feeling groovy. But it is being blinded by these platitudes of light that must also be considered by me in the end. Blinded by that 'power of the highest,' that I must now reconcile with my reality when I come down.

Joseph, do you know where Mary is?

She is out in the stable, frolicking with the power of the highest. You can write a book about it. Call it a gospel. About how Mary had that little lamb. But, I say, your Little Bo Peep is *not* with her sheep. They say it's called, Carpe Diem. Or just putting yourself first. Whatever.
It's also called,

'Use your other fucking hand
to grab the other two birds in the bush!'

…and now you have three, where you only had one. Do It. Do It now. However you Do It, make sure it is before you peak, before the being of light says, 'you must go back and recruit the others.'

Do it, before you feel the urge to tell all your friends that there are actually *twelve* gates into Heaven. Picture that!!! Peter at one. Allah at another. Jehovah at another with Jesus and Baby-Momma peaking around the corner so that all of his believers, who won't know what the …k Jehovah looks like, will get past the 'blind-melon-chitlin.' The Elohim are all stuffed into one gate. Then, let me see, that leaves eight gates for all of the atheists and non-believers.

Do it, before you peak. While you are still feeling good. Feeling blinded. Before you start coming down. 'Jonesing.' As in, Reverend Jim Jones. Persuasion of the masses. Sheep. This usually comes on when you are beginning to come down. When you need others to justify *your* experience.

"Come unto me," they say.
"Believe and be saved."

"...And then I saw this pillar of light..."

Well, that's how addiction happens. Swimming upstream to keep the peak from ending. Pushing more drugs. Another number. Another affair to remember. Another final gathering of the 'righteous'. Another coy forty-five. Another transformation 'fix' to keep the 'transformation' from peaking, ending, coming down.

But one can't argue with reality or Hollywood, sending every passionate build-up scene to commercial when magical fruit and trees of life are involved. Until the next 'happygasm' or good lighting to get you coming back for more. The Creator and the writers must stay employed, you know.

●●●

The *moral* of a feel-good trip or transformation is called,

'Toto'. Todo. Everything. What you think and believe, you can achieve. It's free. Go for it all.

"Even sex?" asked Jean, cynically, as if she were asking that to punish someone.

Jean was the recently 'transformed' wife of my transformation psychotherapist extraordinaire friend, Dean.
She'll 'get' the free love part soon, Dean hopes.

God, I wrote that about Dean yesterday. Today, he announced to me that they are getting a divorce.

●●●

The *message* of a good trip or transformation is,

"You're not in Kansas anymore." Not even.

"Go ask Alice," as Grace Slick said, "I think she'll know."

You're in La La land, Toto. Call it heaven, a good buzz, whatever. See your K-9 friend, Sasha? She is now keenly disguised as the wicked witch of the west. And Whiskers? Isn't he the tin man? And all this from just a bump on the head, as Dorothy found out. Or good acid, as Mr. Leary found out. Or a "touch on the thigh" by an angel, as Jacob of Israel found out. Or, a "deep sleep," as Adam found out.

Hmm. Deep sleep. That's a good one. What a trip! 'Come down,' his rib is missing, and there is a naked woman lying next to him.

I think Adam was 'really' tripping. Passed out. Woke up next to God's wife. God got pissed, and kicked them both out of the garden.
The rib part was just a cover story.

Or, the story may really be about a jealous herb dealer who had a good thing going, creating and selling of every kind of 'sin' semilla herb. Which means 'without seed' herb. 'Sin'. No one could encroach on his deal and germinate herb on their own because the herb that he provided them had no seeds in it. Kind of like gun control. Or the 'only true religion.'

The herb could only be purchased from 'Gods' special garden of virgin, seedless, sin-semilla herb. However, wise old Adam learned how to 'clone,' or take cuttings, while working in God's garden one day. He took a clone from the tree of knowledge. The Mother plant. Mother knows best, you know. From her *side,* he cloned 'Eve.' some of god's good budding female herb.

Then, unfortunately, Adam was booted out of the garden before he could steal pollen from the 'Tree of Life', the Father plant. So, without seeds, and cast out into the lone and dreary world, the family of Adam had to preserve a clone line or bloodline. From cutting to cutting. From clone to clone. Or from Cohen to Cohen, since the original cutting. The 'chosen' family of Adam may just be waiting for that special moment in life when one of their cloned 'first born' (read, 'first cutting') plants miraculously shows as a hermaphrodite, a 'herme.' And all the colored girls sing,

"Doo, doo, doo ."

"... He was a She." As Lou Reed posited. You know the rest. Something about,

An enigmatic "...Walk on the wild side."

A male-female. The messiah. The God-man. The self-contained woman-man. Spontaneously pollinating himself, producing his own seeds, and therefore, the enigmatic, regenerative creating power.

Hmm. A hermaphrodite. Now, isn't this a linguistic conundrum? Given that the Messiah, the mythical Jesus, is known in magical, alchemical and occult circles as an embodiment of Hermes.
Now, that would be a stretch. The part about Hermes. Not the part about the seeds earlier. The Israelites I learned about in the bible were always lying, conniving, cheating, stealing, killing and sacrificing, fornicating, castrating and circumcising all to keep, or to control, or to manipulate, or to demarcate, or to annihilate, genealogical *seeds*.

Yes, I have that story to thank for the scar on my penis. Child mutilation, instead of soap and a washcloth.

●●●

How could I have known that when I was born, the discovery of a penis between my legs had already determined my place in life? To be labeled as unclean. And without further discussion, the offensive thing between my chubby little legs is cut upon, and scarification is dismissed as a cleaner way to live.

Yes, the most blatant form of scarification is accepted today as mainstream. Bitch and moan about my understanding of Semitism? My fucking foreskin was cut off as a "token" of a mythically channeled real estate contract between a mythical homeless wandering Abraham character and his equally mythical "almighty god."
Consider my foreskin and billions of others as the 'good and valuable consideration' that has given this mythical Abraham and all of his circumcised seed the right and title to his "Land of Canaan" for an "everlasting covenant." In reality, paid in-full by the foreskins of every male who has ever been

cut upon and mutilated by this rite of Abraham.

And a holocaust of foreskins and victims are lain at the hymen of a Wailing Wall, at the foot of a homunculus cross, or at the door of a Holy Church, a Holy Temple, a Holy Mosque, a Bridesmaid, a Virgin, whatever.

'And if you're really, really good, and pay me lots of tithing, I will split the swollen virgin mound of Olive and all you scarified believers can plunge in, …and living water will rush out.'

Read the Holy Bible. It's all there. Bloody bed sheets and all. Consummated in enough bloody retribution scare tactics to make believers of any impressionable Sunday school children. On a recent visit with my mother, she reminded me that "We are a covenant people," and then she asked me if I remembered what that meant. Yes mother, I know all too well.

For all I know, the story of Abraham, the father of all circumcision, could have just been an ancient version of 'Silence Of the Lambs.' About an unstable-minded 'Sochet.' Mindfully tending to the sharpness of his sacrificial 'Chalef.' It's special, slender, long blade, gleaming in the light, without a single nick or irregularity. The blades' lambskin leather sheaf, worn from many years of use, kept rolled-up carefully in a bundle of silk.

"Yes, this knife. My favorite knife, for my favorite son. ….Now that I have decided which knife, I can't stop looking at Isaac's neck."

…The voices.

"…and you will be made a father of nations."

And something about "sands." And something about how well little Isaac was groomed. Without asking any questions. Without reading the small print.

…The voices.
"… My son."

…The voices.
…As I take the heavy wood off my small son's back.

…The voices.
"….My son."

…The voices.

…as I wrestle my unwilling son back onto the stack of wood.

…The voices.
>"My son."

…The voices.
…I tie him this time because he keeps getting off.
>"My son."

…More voices. …my fingers trembling with anticipation.

>"My son."

…The voices.

…A goat is bleating softly at Abraham's feet, nibbling on his shoelaces. Breaking one of them.

…Another voice.

…A crafty idea…

"That Billy the Goat, I'll slit his throat."

And, moments later, a shaking, trembling Isaac, is standing next to the blood, the smell, and the flames, trying to make sense of it all. A giddy Abraham, is staring into the same flames, while running the blade back and forth across his thigh. Isaac, still nervous. Still shaking. Thinking his father is crazy. What gave him the clue? Hello! He is hearing voices in his head, telling him to kill Isaac, his own favorite son. "Whom he loved." And his voices did it to 'tempt' him. And we are told, in the story, that this Abraham really did pile on his son the very wood that would burn him. Did he maybe make it hard for him? Maybe mock him? Make his boy stumble? Perhaps hide, in the faggots of wood on Isaac's small back, a waterskin full of homemade beer, for later, after the sacrifice. When he planned to enjoy a smoke and to carefully tend to his Chalef. To make sure that it did not suffer a nick.

O.K., we need more inspired men like that in our community. Just give us our list of commandments. Oh, and our personal revelation from our God. You know, that loving revelation that commands things like,

> 'Utterly destroy them all.
> Men, women and children.'

Forget the symbolic ram in the thicket. That was just gratuitous astrological symbolism for the dawning of the great age of Aries.

Yeah, right. I say absolutely NO figgy pudding from THAT tree. Curse it immediately. So that it "bare no fruit."

Prodigal son, do you know who YOUR daddy is?

"Jesus, son, if you tell ANYONE what really went down between Mary and me, I will forsake you."

•••

But then again, God may just be fronted by the little goofy gray-haired man behind the curtain who dishes out hearts, brains and courage to save God's ass. Then the prophet, shaman, little gray-haired man, takes to the sky in his hot air balloon, chariot, magic carpet, whatever.

•••

And, finally, the only result of this 'transformation' after you come down is…

You get to keep the shoes.

Click them three times.

Believe. Believe. Believe.

8

So, who is this God, literally?

I have been taught that I only use a small portion of my mind. Extraordinary! I will take it, and teach it truths like the Easter Bunny, Santa, The Tooth Fairy, Noah and his Ark, Jonah and that whale, The Great Mystery of Godliness, Falling in Love. Hey, isn't that like the "fall" of Adam? And why don't they say, "the fall of Adam and Eve?"

Eve was frolicking; remember their story? Eating the forbidden fruit. Falling for the snake. Yet it is still just called "the fall of Adam."

Hum? 'The Fall.' Falling into love? Falling from grace? Is falling in love, an original sin? The judgment upon the lovers being that they will inevitably fall, or come down from that grace, and get kicked out of their 'eat of all the trees,' Eden. No more walking naked in the cool of the day. The 'lovers' have to go-it on their own. Thorns. Thistles. Tilling. Sweating husbands, sorrowing wives. Knowing both good and evil times. Until their next fall into love.

Unless, unlike Eve, you're the Virgin Mary,
She lied. The Big One.

"It's my husband's son."

"What apple?"

She didn't get kicked out. We know she got frolicked by the father of Jesus. This is called a 'little white lie.' Don't try to understand. Eve didn't get it. Mary did. Mary's story is in every cathedral. Eve's is in one. She looks like the Pillsbury Doughboy. Wearing, quite unfashionably, a goatskin. All hunched over, and kicked out. Jonesing badly.
Mary, on the other hand, is on the leading edge of fashion. Fair Mabeline skin. Scandinavian features. Royal robes. Lots of shrines and gothic real estate. *She* lied.

The beauty of Mary's little white lie is that we now have Christianity, as we know it. All that Pavlovian peace, love and kindness to their neighbors. Not to mention the overshadowing of maggies, of altar boys, and of heathen nations. And what about all the millions of women, men and children who have been burned, raped, tortured and killed to preserve the sweet message of Christianity? Or any other religion, for that matter. They all seem more like a disease than a blessing. Religions have, in the name of their gods, killed more people than any war or plague.

Perhaps wearing a scarlet letter or being confined to a general quarantine would keep religious zealots away from the rest of humanity where no more of their harm could be perpetrated on non-believers. Where their 'repent or be damned' disease could be kept in child-safe bottles. Far out of the reach of children. Where their own 'true believers' could be commanded to stay in their own private Gardens of Eden, forever.....

OR ELSE THEY WOULD DIE!

Surround them with little baby cherubim and flaming swords to keep them riveted to their own obedient paths. Neuter their love and oneness. Give them fig leaves to hide the shame of their own nature. Give them no way out. That is, no way out except through sex, their nature. And when their innocence is naturally lost, let them leave their Eden and become 'like unto'…the rest of us. Knowing that we are all good, and all evil. No special people. No chosen people.

●●●

It reminds me of the scene in the movie Midnight Express where Brad Davis, God rest his soul, was mentally rotting away in the neutered Eden of a Turkish jail. No one escapes, he is told. And like a good, lobotomized sheep, he too began to walk the wheel of his nightmarish hell. Put on his social fig leaf. That is, until his girlfriend inexplicably shows up for a conjugal visit. Inspiring him to muster the courage to walk against the wheel. To eat the forbidden apple. To get his freedom back from the prison warden god he gave it to. To murder the god of the garden and climb out of his rabbit-hole into the light of a new day.

●●●

Hum? Sex, their nature. "And when the woman saw that the tree was good, …was pleasant, ….was desired, …she took" And all the colored serpents said,

"doo, doo doo."
Ye shall not surely die.
"Take a walk on the wild side."

And Eve wrestled out her salvation with a snake, a consensual pretzel, or supposedly none of us would be here. Lot's own daughters wrestled with his sacred snake, over a fine bottle of wine (hum?). The concubines of the mythical Abraham wrestled with several of his snakes on behalf of Sarah. And Solomon, the Wilt Chamberlain of all times, shed his skin with hundreds of willing concubines to give himself the inspiration to build a temple to his god. The god of what? The god of sexual deviance? Other men's wives for himself, concubines for his prophets and male child mutilation to weed out his competitors? Pretty much describes most any king of the forest. King of the pit stop. King of the world. Whatever.

●●●

God sent fire from heaven for all the sodomic sexual deviants. Deviance is only O.K. if it is done for 'God's sake.' Like Noah violating his daughters, then getting drunk and passing out naked in front of his sons. Or, like Lot, giving his daughter to the angry Sodomites to be 'deviated' with so that he could save the life of God's handsome visiting angel instead.
Or how about the King David story, a little voyeurism to inspire the prophet of God? He basically has the hots for a married woman.

Started going 'commando' as he jogged in his kilt past 'Shebie's' house. He'd often let his snake peer over his balcony into Bathsheba's private shower. Deciding then to take what was pleasant to him. Even going to the extent of killing Bathsheba's lover, and then sequestering her in his home.

You know, this was the same House of David through whose loins the baby Jesus descended, as the story goes. Like father, like son. Or, like father, like 'son of God.'

A little bit of foreshadowing, I mean overshadowing. Hell, just call it adultery. May as well keep indiscretion in the family. Our model citizens. But kick those wicked capitalists out of the temple, for God's sake! They are changing money, when they should be slaughtering animals and birds. Sprinkling blood. An everlasting plume of death and slaughter rising day and night towards …whom else? That's right. Their god. For God's sake! Can you imagine the stench? Have you ever been to a slaughterhouse? Only imagine wagonloads of sacrifices. A holy Auschwitz, if you will. If that offends you, blame it on the apple.

NYC
The Edenic apple
Pressing against the teeth

CHOKING GOD

Of humanity
The apple
Taking its metaphorical fall
As in drop
From the very beginning
A lesson in symbolism
Dying
For the sins of the world
The apple
That sacre coeur
Nailed to a tree
Off the head of his son
What does William Tell?
Pierced in its side
It's the fucking apple
That has been blamed
For giving mankind
Unkind knowledge
Of good and evil
Ah yes
The capitalistic dream
Of juicy red sweetness
The Big Apple
Bite me
Taste me
Eat me
Sleep
And twin trees come down
While the mirrors
In Washington
Declare

Who's the fairest of them all?
The Middle East is the fairest
The Middle East has the oil
I cannot tell a lie
Our presidents say
I thought the mirror
Was saying, 'hash oil'
And doped up Georgie boys
Start whacking down cherry trees
With the approval of congress
Of course
And axes are bloodied
While the collectivist pig
Feasts on tea
And cherry pie

You see, our model citizens are still tabulating sacrifices and acceptable losses to justify their indiscretions and addictions. Keeping it all in the family. Using "god bless America" as their political platform to gain the hearts, minds and sensibility of the religious voters. Voters who, instead of turning their proverbial cheek, turn instead a blind eye to heathen sacrifices in far away lands. Women and children bleeding oil out of their veins to satiate a new economic future, one *they* can't afford. Sold to us by these crony capitalists. And, for god's sake, their audacity!

•••

READ ME. And so I did. That's why I don't believe in Gods. I'm a believer in small print.

> "And he was clothed with a vesture dipped in blood, and his name is called the Word of God."

It says this. Literally! Every God that man has written about wears this same vesture. Different blood. Same story. Now I get the picture. If I'm really, really good, I'll be given extra wine and cheese in my heaven's mansion. Just stick to the Word of God. You know. That *one* interpretation. Just follow the blood.

I've seen Bibles where the words spoken by God are literally printed in red ink.

So, who is this God, literally?

I look around me, and I see flowers, and trees, and joy, and sadness, and I am told God is in all these things. I look, and I notice I continue to see flowers, and trees, and joy, and sadness. I have yet to see, God.
Some say it is because God is All-Powerful, or All-Knowing, or In Spirit, or Omnipresent. I have yet to meet "All-Powerful." I have yet

to meet "All-Knowing." I have yet to see "In Spirit." I have yet to meet "Omnipresent."

If there is a perfect God who is in everything, He's hanging out on St. John's Island. Swimming in the aqua blue water. Building heavenly sandcastle mansions on the fabulous coral-white spotless beaches. Nude sunbathing. Getting his hair corn-braided, after getting his toenails painted by Jezebel. He's turning water into wine. Eating lots of bread and fish. An eternal flamer. Walking on water to Isla Tortola and St. Thomas. And he is calling *that* reality.

Never mind the whole thing about heaven. He could see that one coming. Millions of 'holier than thou' ingrates sitting on his lap to inherit their chunk of celestial suburbia. Sorting out the whole mess. Getting all his costumes right. Black skin, white skin, fake beards. Technicalities like,

"My right, is your left."

Arguing points of commandments with self-righteous know-it-alls. Law mongers. Getting the right reward with the right level of forgiveness, humility, and repugnance.

Oh, and all that catching up to do with our sequestered Mother in Heaven. You know, letting her out of the closet. Admitting that it is She who wears the pants in their Godship. And, admitting to her that he feels like a chump. For not pulling-out in time when he overshadowed Mary. And for losing their ratings to a suppositious child and his birth mother.

●●●

I consider myself to be a spiritual person. I feel compelled to seek the mystical answers to life, creation, relation, and emotion. I'm Capricorn, my Berkeley friend, a Leo, reminds me.

Now, I've never met or seen God. But I can't say that I have never met Jesus. I have. In my closet one night. Under a large olive tree, next to a meandering path. I ended up weeping at his feet. Somewhere between the dirty socks and the sweaters. It was a beautiful experience. I could tell you about it. But you wouldn't believe me. Trees don't grow in closets.

In my seeking, I've felt like the donkey. Continually walking towards the carrot dangling just beyond my nose. There is a carrot. Figuratively. Even when I don't want to notice, it's still there, dangling. In the name of Oneness. Love. Equality. The All. Source. The Universe. Any one of a number of New Age titles that subtly replace the concept of God with a pseudo, Eastern philosophy mixed with tantric sex and cowboy boots. Illusion mongers. Reality mongers. Taunted by our pre-libidinous immaturity. *Everyone* sees a carrot. *Feels* a carrot. Some want to believe that they will *eat* carrots, forever, in one reality or another. And I applaud them. I love the seeming science of faith and its subsequent miracles.

Santa came to my two daughters last Christmas. They knew he would.

9

"For answer, see other side."

Cassy, after reading some of my manuscript, tells me I sound pissed off. Maybe I am. I told myself that I wasn't. That I was O.K. now. Really. That I had transformed. That I had let go. My thoughts were saying, "Come on in now the water is fine." I am beyond anger. I am beyond hate. I have forgiven everybody. I am recruiting now. I am swallowing my pills. The being of light has told me to go back and get the others. So, I am writing to you.

But my cynicism tells me otherwise,. That I have given up on lilies. That I am on the left hand of God now. That I am toiling. And sowing. I'm not hoping to get 'arrayed' anymore. The lilies never knew I was considering them anyway. I found that lilies are like sunsets and Mother Nature. They'll just array themselves anyway. Water seeks its own level.

I, however, need to be considered. When Cassy told me I sounded pissed, I realized that perhaps I am. I want my anger to do something for me. I want to charge my actions against my *forgiveness* card. The one that pays back three percent on all purchases. Gives me bonus sky miles. Builds my mansions in the sky. Yes, my mansion in the sky. I was checking it out one day and found God frolicking in my garden with Mary. They were not interested in building my mansion at all. They were in the lilies. Considering. Not sowing. Not toiling. The carpenter was sleeping. Serpents were plucking forbidden fruit. It was all very overshadowing. And confusing.

The small print had read "Lakefront property." "Swimming pool." "Jogging paths." "Gated community." I know it said, "Gated community." "Covenants and restrictions." I had read the advertisement many times. Only I would have the pass. Someone was supposed to knock. I was supposed to answer. There was to be no doorknob on the outside of the door. No doorbell. A no soliciting sign. Saviors were to stay outside on the porch knocking.

But some porridge had definitely been eaten. Beds had been slept in. Virgins with no oil were coming in by some other way. Animals that definitely were *not* on the Ark were disrupting my builders, two by two. Construction was way behind. Whales were washed up on the beach, and Jonah was nowhere to be found. I was pissed. I was peaking. And I wanted to grab two birds in the bush before I came down. Beat my demon to the ground. I tried using what credit I believed I had on my *forgiveness* card to keep the builders working. I may as well have left home without it.

Cassy is right. I do sound pissed. The water isn't turning to wine. Does this all sound very confusing? Don't try to understand. Keep reading. Let it distill upon you like dew. A chemical wedding. A philosopher's stone. A Holy Grail. A Yellow Brick Road. Click them three times. The shoes. You are wearing the shoes, aren't you?

Believe. Believe. Believe.

How can I forgive God and Mary when they are in every cathedral? It would seem kind of silly, wouldn't it? I can just see it now. It would look like a scene in the movie Schindler's List. The one where the German commandant, portrayed by Ralph Fiennes, is pronouncing 'forgiveness' upon his death camp Jews.

"I forgive you." "I forgive you."

As he decided which ones he would flippantly kill and those he would let live. His forgiveness card was obviously sacrilegious. I could see the indifferent sincerity in his mocking eyes like he wanted to be acknowledged for acting like a saint or a Santa. "This one's for you." "And this one's for you." Forgiving them. Granting them absolution from his killing machine. Absolved of all their emaciated human being.

And then here I am, forgiving deities from behind the comfort of my beam, and casting a first stone at the mote of my God's mythical novelty.

God and Mary, I forgive you. For not building my mansion. For playing in my garden. For not solving world hunger. For not creating world peace. For allowing me to keep the shoes. For commanding that I be baptized when I was much too young to understand the complicated nature of original sin. See, I just became cynical again. That's not forgiveness. Ask God. He knows everything. You won't find Him at my heavenly mansion, though. Neither one of them exists.

What if it really had been true? That my heavenly beachfront property really wasn't just blue sky. But, I've seen the Word of God. It's a bloody sheet. Robe. Vesture. Whatever. The double meanings only work for priests, kings, and tithe collectors.

●●●

So, I am pissed. Pissed at myself. Perhaps my own beliefs needed choking. It was all my own doing. I mean the shoes. The believing. The mansions. The right hand of God. The sacrificial hike with my father and mother to the path of the religious altar. All that wood, a token ram in the thicket for measured obedience. Glorious eventuality. It all sounded so very exciting. Angels. Mansions. Villains. Bad guys. A fair virgin.

How quickly our hearts become the master. Pumping faster. When that which is against life or challenges reality and is inside the great 'What If' draws one in so skillfully. But time, as in tie me, as in bind me down, is the only thing that forgives so seldom; it's never. Time is ruthless. It cheats behind your back. It cheats behind mine. Like retrograde, and leap year. Time is behind everything. It hangs on tenaciously to each 'would have' and 'what if.' And 'what if's' keep no promises. A 'what if' turns to its beloved and says,

"I might die to you tonight."

All in the name of a cheap little heartbeat.

●●●

Jenny, my client, is getting married. She is going to Jamaica on her honeymoon. She tells me she is so excited because she has never actually seen the ocean. What if the ocean is not there when she arrives?

I've never been to China. Yet, I believe it exists. Isn't that the classic recruiting tool for a belief in God? I've never seen God, either. Should I believe in Him? Where are my shoes? Where is my faith? Faith is in my closet, under the tree with Jesus, next to the sweater.

My friend has been to China. To study Chinese medicine. He told me all about it. He is six foot two. Tall, blonde, blue eyes, handsome. In small towns people would surround him because he spoke Chinese. They wanted to know about America and to have their photo taken with him. He was like a God to them.

In one town, he feared for his life because the people got agitated when he wanted to walk away from their curiosity. Some had formed a line and had been waiting with their cameras ready for an hour. They held him, literally. He was on the front page of the town newspaper. My friend, Matt. Walking in a China I've never seen, became like a God.

Jesus, the Son of a god, on the other hand, walked all over Israel, Egypt, Rome, Greece, and Turkey, and sailed the Mediterranean. Supposedly, he did miracles. Raised the dead. Healed the sick. Created bread. Created fish. Walked on water. Walked into the temple of Jerusalem. Kicked out the bankers. Had a new star made just for himself.

And yet, he was not on the front page. Not even the local section or the obituaries. Until seventy years after he died. How cute! No one gave a shit. Not even one contemporary slime ball news reporter. The tabloids, perhaps? NO!

Mathew, seven decades, and several yawns later, made a reference to him in a letter. An opportunity-seeking postal worker kept it, along with all the other letters he was purloining from Mark, Luke and John. He got them published, and now we have the immutable New Testament.

Mary, Joseph, Judas Priest, and Jesus H. Christ all on a popsicle stick for your 'historical' convenience.

Or was it a cross?

Or a tree?

Whatever.

It did have a funny riddle printed on it:

KING OF THE JEWS

The small print read,

<blockquote>"For the answer, see the other side."</blockquote>

I looked on the other side and I saw a small rabbit, with a pocket watch. And I asked myself, "Do rabbits carry pocket watches?" I was curious. So, I decided to follow the rabbit to ask him. I found myself falling down this long tunnel. And I noticed a bottle. I looked to see if it read,

POISON.

It was only labeled,

DRINK ME.

So, I found myself drinking. Oh no! The small print! I forgot to read the small print. Something about,

> 'My ways not being his ways,'

And.
> '...NO other gods before me,'

And,

'...Bloody this.' And, 'Bloody that,'

And,

> '...Bloody soiled vestures.'

Then, I came to a door. And it was labeled,

> "DO NOT GO BACK
> AND GET THE OTHERS."

I wake up. And I find myself crammed inside this teeny tiny house. My arms and legs sticking out of the doors and windows. I am wearing my own conditioning. Obviously beyond its time. Can you blame me for my cynicism? Even if you do, I hope you find it entertaining. Me, well, I'm still looking for my 'right-hand' piece of mushroom so I may reduce my ego to a convenient enough size that I may walk out the front door of my conditioning without any attachment to it.

As for 'the others?' Well, who are they anyway? And can they quote,

> "How doth the little busy bee?"

And who am I? Which reminds me of this conversation I had with myself.

> I look into the mirror
> To see the monkey on my back
> The monkey on my back, is me
> Then who's back am I on?
> Upon Whom's back, I am
> Who's back?
> Yes, Who, is Whom
> And whom, is I
> Whom, is Who?
> Yes, and, I is also
> I, got on Who's back
> And Who, is Whom

●●●

So, you see, clearly, I am in no position to 'get others.' My understanding of life's riddles is still questionable. Yet I do it anyway. I try to get 'them' to follow. Just like

Jesus did. He was the greatest recruiter of all time.

…As the story goes.

"Come to me."

He would say.

I always had to shut my eyes on that part.

…You know, in the movie Jungle Book. The part where Ka the snake is wooing the lost man-child Mowgli up into, of course, the Tree Of Life. There, he would temptingly sing,

"Trust in me…"   (His enticing eyes).
"Slip into.. slumber…" (His slithering voice).
"Slowly your senses…" (His lullaby tongue).
"Cease to resist…"   (His smothering tail).

It was always too hypnotic. Somewhat creepy. It felt like warm bathwater lasting forever. You see, Mr. Disney's bible puts Jesus' words into the mouth of a snake, where they properly belong. Slithering and enticing. Just like the imposter 'Almighty God' of the Garden of Eden, who gives commandments, and gives 'names.' Limiting. Boxing in. How could the 'limitless God in everything' place limits on himself in Adam? Quite a conundrum.

The true 'God of The Garden,' dressed as the phantom operatic snake, acting like a philanthropic Johnny Appleseed, could not hold himself back from giving EVERYTHING to Adam and Eve.

Well, first to Eve. God is love. Remember?

•••

Ever wonder why so many cultures feature serpents as God? As sources of the Wisdom Knowledge? Or why do other cultures subtly twist the serpent of giving and healing into a snake of temptation and evil? Or, why did Moses hold up a brazen snake for the Children of Israel to follow?

"You can have it all,"

Was the battle cry.

"So, you shall plunder,"

…gold and silver from the Egyptians.

"Then, ye shall possess,"

Lands from others who are living in them.

...The voices.
>"Kill."

...Even the children?

"...Utterly."

...The voices.
>"Kill."

...Even the women?

>"Destroy."

...Them all? Man, woman, child?

>"Utterly!. ...and I mean utterly!"

And it will last forever...

Yeah well, clearly *that* God is still tripping. He is still doing his job and 'getting the others' to "come to me." To 'love the Lord, thy god',

before anything else.

…Even before one's own child? One asks.

"Yes, obviously."

"You should have thought about that before sending your unfavored concubine Hagar with your unfavored son Ishmael away into the desert with just a skin full of water."

"But, …but,"

"…He's my only son, and well, my other wife Sarah is one-hundred years old…"

"Do you think I give a fuck if he is your only son?

"…Jeeesus Chrrrist!!"

10

Hippos swallow snakes, swallowing hippos.

What is all the same fucking thing, man? The thing, that never fucking happens, tomorrow? The thing, that one must hold on to, in the moment? Not, "like" it's your last moment in your life," as Janice Joplin so urgently urged. But instead, hold on to, *because* it's the last moment in your life. Each moment uniquely is, was, the last. And it's just too damn "heavy man", as she said, to try to hold a moment after the fact.

"The fucking thing, man," Janice said,

"You gotta call it love."

The ninety-seven percent gamble. She, too, is still tripping. Somewhere. Out there. Recruiting. Perhaps we should listen again to the rest of her album. To the part where she sings, how love grabs hold, like drizzling rain, "like a ball and chain." Like a dangling carrot. She is cool and confusing at the same time. Kind of like my thoughts, when I am tripping. Or Alice's English, when she is tripping. It is all the same thing. Over. And over. And over.

Except for this one time. I don't know how it happened. Except that I was tripping. All of a sudden, Matt was in my head. I mean, inside my head. And I was inside his. For a brief moment in time, what he was seeing and feeling, and what I was seeing and feeling, were as if we were looking out of each other's eyeballs. Feeling each other's sensations. Having each other's thoughts. It was cool and unsettling at the same time. I didn't know how long Matt was going to be in my head. Or if I would ever have my own private head back again. It was weird. It happened a few times after that. Each time, neither he, nor I knew how to make it happen. There was no 'going back to get the others." The 'other' was already in my head, having my same thoughts. That was definitely NOT "the same fucking thing." Whatever happened to "my thoughts are not your thoughts, neither are your ways my ways?" Another conundrum.

"You gotta call it love,"

…She reminds me. Love will explain the carrots in life.

Blame it on love
I thought we had an understanding
Blame it on love
I thought it was what you wanted

Blame it on love
I didn't know it would hurt you
Blame it on love
You wouldn't understand
Blame it on love
You said you wouldn't tell
Blame it on love
But you promised
Blame it on love
I need, I need, I need

I feel that love is the way I think things are. Love is my titillation with that way. Love is my interpretation of things. Love is my anticipation. My predetermination. My absentmindedness. My drunkenness with my own obsession. Love is my hunger for new information. Love is my desire to forgive, to be sorry. Love is being what I meant. Or what I said. Or what I meant, I said. Any of my natural survival mechanisms built into my psyche to get me to the next cheap little heartbeat. Yes, the little heartbeat.

Thump, thump, thump.
As I follow my rabbits.
Thump, thump.
What I meant, was…
Thump, thump.
"Don't stop, don't stop."
… thumping.

The love mantras chortle as we eat each other's dangling carrots. Hearts pumping faster. Love and oneness oozing. Peaking. The being of light.

BAM!

Oh God! The wizard's hat, the carrot. The broomsticks. The bathwater. Apples, snakes. Blame it on love? Love doesn't give a shit. Love turns to its beloved and says,

"I will die for you tonight,"

…all in the name of cheap little heartbeats.

Am I to be responsible for someone's love for me? Are they to be responsive to my love for them? Love is a million different languages spoken at once. "I love you" can mean a million different things to a million different lovers.

Show me love,
I'll show you a motion.
Call it love.
I'll call it devotion.

Devotion to one's self. Lovers are wanters. "I love you" translates to "my wants are taken care of right now as you keep doing exactly what you are doing." To find out how to love another, find out what they want. Love what they want. Love their wants that you are with.

How much more daring would it be to say, "I'm getting my wants now, Baby," instead of the obsequious "I love you?" Which could mean anything from "I really want to just jump your bones," to "Do you want to hear my latest ideas on furniture arrangement?" All the sadness from all the broken-hearted lovers in the world will not bring understanding to them or to their loved ones. The objects of the desire.

So, what's the use? I can sit on my ass, look up to the sky, and lo and behold, my carrot swings right into my mouth. I CAN have my cake and eat it too. After all, it's my party. My lonely party called expectation. And I don't have to do a damn thing but just sit on my ass, put my nose up in the air, and devour my dangling carrot expectations.
Kind of like a snake. Snakes are lousy lovers. Coiled and waiting for love to happen. Snakes only say "I love you" as they are dislocating their jawbone to swallow you whole. It's actually quite a beautiful process. Like a love poem.

Let me slither in your grass
Let me turn the blade aside
Let me lay your body down
Let me on your tenseness glide
Let me peek into your cavern
Let me poison all your fears
Let me sink my fangs into them
Let me swallow down your tears
Let me laugh at your confession
Let me hiss at all your pain
Let me smother my apologies
Let me do it all again
Let me watch my magic in you
Let me tighten up your breath
Let me visit you in dreamtime
Let me fatten in your death
Let me coil in your shadows
Let me digest in your sun
Let me flick the flesh that hides you
Let me own you when I'm done

●●●

Now puppies, as in puppy love, on the other hand, do not wait for love to happen. I was driving on the interstate the other day, and I saw a billboard sign that consisted of a man's legs from the waist down, with a little puppy dog humping the man's leg. The caption read,

CHOKING GOD

"Spay or neuter your pet."

Oh yes, they call it puppy love. But I don't see any billboard signs that say, "spay or neuter your lover." Because true love doesn't hump someone's leg. Love dislocates its jaw, slowly and patiently and then swallows the leg. Like a snake. But a tame one. A hippo snake. A nimble swimmer. A poker face. Solid, man.

Hippos swallow snakes, swallowing hippos.

Any time I parade my sorry story in the name of "But I did it for love"; you can bet I wasn't getting what I really wanted, and that the object of my 'love' wasn't clued in. True love is getting what I want, remember? If I remember that love is ME getting what I want, and then loving the want that I'm with, then I will also know that any sorry love story I tell is really me just being angry at myself for being a 'good dog,' a 'puppy-lover,' humping the leg of my lover, not getting what I want, and then saying it was loves fault. True love doesn't chase sticks, hump legs, or get locked in bathrooms. True love is three birds in two hands and none in the bush. No looking back. No lacking. No unfulfilled wants.

But then, who am I to share missives with you about what love is or isn't? Love is a million different things to a million different lovers. Love is that fine bottle of wine you always talk of opening, and then do, because time just got better now! Eventuality, is happening now!. The perfect gamble. Doubling down. Tipping over into its novelty. Love un-mysterious. A universal constant, figured. Love conditional. Love certain. Not given freely. Not like that guy who gave 365 valentine cards to his lover on Valentine's Day. Not like the yappy dog who sniffs everyone's crotch and is so eager and excited that he urinates on your Persian rug.

Love not given out to the neighbor. Love given instead, 'as' to oneself. *That* love, IS loving one's neighbor. Not sloppy. Love, as if, for my authentic self. A perfect gamble.

So, how do I know if I am smothering or humping my lover? Or relying on a belief beyond its useful life. How do I avoid ending up on a goofy billboard?

Hippo life. Remember? You won't see a hippo humping someone's leg. Or wagging its tail for acknowledgement. Want what I want. Love the want I'm with, and remember the words of Boston, one of my favorite high school bands, "Don't look back."

●●●

Well, I am looking back again…to finish my story.

God! I feel like a ghost. Like I'm in another body looking out at life. Like there is this whole part of me that is completely gone, I feel like I can look and see, as if through a pane of glass, a memory of a life I know I lived in, loved, and was consumed and wholly entreated by. Fellow believers, common persuasions, respected for my knowledge of the bible. What brought about my unplugging? So subtly that only now am I looking back and seeing how completely consuming that life was. Hell, I'm writing this, in my starched shirt and tie, reflecting on the consequences and rewards of my unplugging.

I loosen up my tie. I feel hunched over. Kicked out. I was tasting the fruit in the religious garden. Eating from all of the trees. Climbing all of the mountains. Kayaking every stream. Following every rainbow. Till I found my…dream? Yes! It must have been all a dream. Or, 'just a thought' as my New

Ager friends suppose. Clearly, I am toiling now. By the sweat of my own brow. Flaming swords of reality. Thorns, thistles, and noxious weeds.

But I know, if I'm really, really good to my mentalisms, affirmations, faith and positive thinking, I could be tasting similar fruit again. I could be climbing similar heaven's gates. Kayaking a river of boundless love. Lords, gods, miracles, blessings. Spooning every rainbow's colors. Sliding down into pots of gold. Feasting on extra wine and cheese. Silver linings behind every cloud.

Jesus! Wouldn't you know it? There is not a single cloud in the sky. Not a single rainbow. No wine and cheese. No heaven's gate. Years of religious education. Countless hours of bible study and seminary. Now, it is just me. In a starched shirt and tie. Laced up business shoes. Day timer. Briefcase. Cell phone. Empty promise from a can of 'genuine king'…of beers. Sunset. Sunglasses. Pen. Paper. Period.

Is it the pen I am waiting for? Or my mind?
I think I am thinking
The cavity of my head has the words
The thoughts, the emotions in it
Sometimes, I relate to a saltshaker

CHOKING GOD

So much salt. Yet so few holes
I've seen coconuts smashed open on rocks
Violated by nails and hammers
Hewn open by blade
For the succulent, tongue-wetting juice
Getting inside. Just under the skin
The fruit of my head begs to be eaten
Split. Peeled
Exaggerated on a plate, in a neat little pile
Called homemade. Come and get it
Press me, into your lips, your mouth
Thank God for salivation
I've come again to be baptized
In your juices
On tongues of angels. Sweet Jesus
To slither down
The straight-narrowness of your throats
Cast myself about
In the crookedness of your flesh
And bury my soul
In the bowels of your starvation
Pop. Sizzle. Fizz
Die…gestion
While you sleep, walk, talk
About how I am in you!
Rolled out
Pricked about
Crossed with a T
The holy Jonah fiber ball
Cleansing out the whale of your soul
Drunken with the acideous wine

Of your spongy spike-innards
Pressing dross against my silent lips
I cry, "my God!"
You have miss taken me
I am finished
Forsaken into the whited sepulchers
Of your septic graveyards
You wash your hands of my pith
That was your bread of life
And I fatten my ears
With your bended knee
Thank thee's, bless that
While I recycle myself in your pollution
And whisper my promise to you all…
I will come back to you again!

Oh yes, I get to keep all of the memories, the coy forty-fives, of *those* shoes.

Whether I want to or not. They are my bread of life. My sacred cow. My dangling carrot. Giving me faith and hope when I least expect it. Courage when I most expect it. And they are my consolation prize when I come just short of it.

The shoes are built into my subconscious mind. Programmed to slither down my throat and look for ways to cause me happiness. The survival of my species. The Bob Barker of my creativity. Always tempting me with the two birds in the bush in exchange for the one bird in my hand. To double down. Bet my bottom dollar. Throw everything to chance. Disguised as faith or trust. Disguised as winging it. Disguised as confidence. To look behind door number two with all the faith, hope, trust and benevolence that I can muster. Never mind the little reality devil on my left shoulder shouting into my ear,

"…You *will* lose yourself
in the service of others."

"Your faith without works *is* dead."

"Really consider the lilies."
"They are working their asses off to eke out their existence on the rocky hillsides of Jerusalem."

"Toiling not' is bullshit…. "

But, the angel of possibilities on my right shoulder, keeps dishing out promises, hope, and discount blessings. Overbooking the commuter flight to heaven. Extra bags of peanuts, of course. No overhead luggage space. I'll have to cram all of my personal preferences into the confessionally small leg space down there by my shoes. No doubt I am wearing them on this flight. Thinking of all the possibilities.

•••

We humans have a voracious appetite for survival. Not the survival of all species, sadly. Just the survival of the accumulated knowledge in each of our little heads. The problem is that we know far too much to save our own knowledge. Just like the little 'HAL' in 2001: A Space Odyssey, we are indifferent to all of the havoc wreaked by our tunnel vision survival mechanism. Aware only of our supremacy. Our wants and desires far surpass our own reality's ability to cope.

You've heard the saying, "If the shoe fits, wear it." I say if the shoe fits, I am peaking. That's when the 'bread of life' is coming to me. When my mother natural self fucks me up the ass with a blessing, a bonus, a miracle. When the shoe fits, your Freudian 'id' has mastered your survival. In that moment, has rewarded you for your idiom. Kind of late to decide what's O.K. and what's not at this late moment.

Karma is living in one's now. Not blaming ones now, on some recompense for ones 'back then.' How predictively boring. Karma is what is *happening* now. Live in it. You asked and received. Don't look back. Don't figure it out. Don't make 'thank you' lists an hour long in the middle of your grammatical Kodak moment. Just remember your cues and every single thing the good witch on your right shoulder says. Look into the camera. The moment won't last forever. One day you too may end up on the left-hand of each god.

The thing is, that when you actually enter Oz's doors, you've peaked. Literally peeked behind the curtain. Things have to start making sense pretty quickly. The left-hand wants to know what the right-hand has been doing along the yellow brick road. And the dog in me will hump the answer out from behind the curtain, closet, whatever. Be careful what you wish or pray for; you might get it. Tierra firma. Home to Kansas. Thorns, thistles. Lone and dreary worlds.

So why keep your nose in the poppy fields? Because, like our own psyche, MGM studios realized that The Yellow Brick Road doesn't exist without a little opiate between the cheek and gums. In the form of trust, faith, hope or lots of fairy dust.

What I 'come down' to after my tunnel-of-white-light visits to Oz, or to heaven, is my trust, faith, and hope that I started with. Plus, either a happy ending, or a less happy ending. Some refer to that added little treat in the end as my 'results.'

The message to myself is to remember that my results are what I live with. Not the idealistic trust, faith or hope. Results are my reality now. My foundation. What I actually have on my feet. The accumulated sweetness of my life. My photographic memories. My own happiness or pleasure in my self. These shoes I keep are my reality.

Growing up, being taught to live for tomorrow, for the better life, I personally had my nose stuck so far up my God's ass that it took years of drugs and a daily high to bring me down. Down from my mentalisms that motivated me by guilt or denial today…for a reward tomorrow. When reality then bit me on the heel, I was left smoldering in all my personal drainage, from which I had expected to be saved by my personal savior.

11

Sackcloth and ashes.

Let's see, where am I? Thank you for being my lyrical therapist and for allowing me to write to you. My psyche is healing again. I can tell. I tend to get cynical when my pills aren't taking effect. As if I, like Jean, am blaming someone for all of the unlyrical moments in my life.

God, I wrote that about myself yesterday. Today, my pills are taking effect.

God. Wouldn't it be great if blaming actually worked? If I really could blame something or someone for every unlikable aspect or action in my life? Every pain. Every sorrow. Gone! With just a short 'blame' mantra. It could even include the silent mantras. The ones that blame silently while the other person is sleeping or watching TV or reading a book. But then it goes a little deeper. Could one just belt out a 'blame' mantra and walk away? Walk away without watching the specter of guilt or hate annihilate the other person? Reason says yes. Ego says no. Because blame, like forgiveness, is also lying to (or cheating) my ego. The forgiveness mantra comes from the 'idea' of a God and a common good. The blame mantra comes from the 'idea' of scapegoats. Also, a lie.

If one believes, or loves, or blames, or forgives, I've found that few walk the road less traveled. The road that expels the mantra and then walks away, content. Most often, expectation immediately follows. One begins subtly looking for the reward for their belief. One begins subtly wanting something back from the object of their love. One subtly wants to see their scapegoat suffer thirst in the desert for their blame. One wants to see the sackcloth and ashes on their forgiven.

•••

The forgiveness mantra, supposedly works like a cute little veil of forgetfulness. Yeah, right. Like a magic aspirin pill. 'Extra strength forgiveness' for those annoying 'forget-me-nots' that don't seem to go away. 'Night-time strength forgiveness' that works away at those vile memories of what you have forgiven while you are asleep. You don't have to do a damn thing. Except just wake up in the morning. See, I'm smiling and happy now, just like in the commercial.

●●●

The other mantra, called blame, supposedly puts a Star of David on the object of your 'final solution.' Marking it for slaughter. The problem is that blame doesn't account for the little Annie Franks of reality hiding between the walls of resistance of the one being blamed.

It reminds me of a talk show I was listening to that was poking fun at unusual state laws. Turns out there is a law in Michigan requiring manufacturers of knee and elbow pads to display on their packaging a disclaimer that the protective pads will only protect the parts of the body actually covered by the protective pads. Some blame mongers, narcissists most certainly, had sued manufacturers for bodily injuries not meant to be protected by their padding. Can you believe that? Like those who carelessly press a wad of gum to the bottom of each table at the malt shop. Adding to the bubblegum-braille poetry that regurgitates their equally careless fingers. Does one really put their blame onto a scapegoat and then have their anger or judgement just disappear? Without secretly staying awake to watch for its return from the desert, heavily laden with the punishment that was 'deserved?'

●●●

Here's a lesson in metaphor. Hitler blamed the Jews. The Jews put their blame on unblemished goats. The Adam in all of us, who named the goat, blamed Eve. The Eve in all of us blamed the serpent. The serpent just had a plan. And the Eve in all of us responded to it, so the story goes. That's why blame is a lie. We learned that the forbidden fruit was eaten. We know it was the Eve in all of us who ate it out of the hand of the snake.

If the character Eve could have just said,

> "O.K. God, I wanted a delicious apple,
> and took it when it was offered to me."

> "I love hanging out and eating your fruit."

> "Cain is not my husband's son.".

> "Oh, and by the way,
> I loved every minute of it."

Perhaps our Adams and Eves would not be cast out of love's shack. Perhaps our Cain's would not have killed our Abel's. Perhaps Moses, with his brazen serpent, would not have killed all those Egyptians in the Red

Sea. Perhaps the twelve tribes would not have "utterly destroyed" villages of men, women and children for their God. The Israelites would not have felt compelled to kill millions of animal sacrifices. The Hitlerites would not have been compelled to kill any Israelites. And a linguistical 'Adolf and Eva' would not have been compelled to poison-apple themselves in their Edenic Reich land. All because of original lies. Original sins.

BLAME.

That's perhaps why I can't honestly forgive the Gods and Marys in my life. I really would rather stay angry at them in order to mask the realization I have that my belief in them didn't give me what I expected. And my ego doesn't want to take responsibility for my own over-expectation.

I'm rambling again. Skip ahead if you need to. Entertainment is what you make of it.

12

Eating Timothy.

A knock came at the door. It was Christmas day. We weren't expecting any visitors, other than Santa, who had obviously already come and gone. My two little daughters were busy playing 'make believe' with their newly acquired toys.

Note to myself: Isn't it funny how we call childhood playing, 'pretend', or 'make believe,' while at the same time portending Santa, Jesus and virgin births as reality? Immaculate conception giving birth to immaculate deception?

Earlier that morning, I had overheard my young daughters discussing the origin of a "My Little Pony" toy. Like two Darwinian philosophers positing on the origin of species. "I got that from Santa." "Did not." "Did so." "Did not,....See? It says 'made in China on the bottom," said my youngest. I could see the wheels turning in the sweet mind of my seven-year-old as the China label redefined her North Pole logic. Like the bones of Lucy unraveling the biblical Adam. Ecclesiastical me to the rescue. I told them

Santa has many helpers in China. An outright lie to preserve the mystery of Santa for yet a couple more years.

Meanwhile, despotic leaders wink at the horror of sweatshops where seven-year-olds work twelve-hour days to make toys for all the good little boys and girls of the world. Talk about the origin of species?. Their tiny bones help fill up corporately gained, Pol Pot graveyards. Their strawberry killing fields labeled appropriately, "Made in China." Packaged in the aptly sung words of Lennon, "Living is easy with eyes closed." Ignorance is bliss. Meanwhile, deception will go on stuffing Santa's sleigh like so much unprotected sex so that consumers worldwide can get their jollies. Perhaps accurate product labeling would re-sensitize humanity. "Made by sweating seven-year-olds in China." "60% rayon, 40% starvation, and 16 ounces of toxic pollution."

•••

One crisp fall, my Christian relatives had come from their ranch to visit for the holidays and wanted to cook for all of us a cultural Passover meal just like the Israelites in the bible. Complete with bitter herbs, figs, dates, nuts, honey, and a fattened lamb, unblemished and shanked, by well-intending, non-kosher cooks. The only blemish was the truth. My youngest daughter asked them where the meat came from. When my relatives answered, "It was a biblical *tradition* to eat lamb," my daughters wouldn't eat it. Couldn't eat it. On the level of truth, my daughters knew that this particular lamb was Timothy. Timothy was a doggie, a runt baby lamb that my relatives had taken in when there was 'no room for him in the inn'.

A doggie is what my grandma called a third extra baby lamb in a litter. Often, these would be rejected by the mother. Usually, they starve to death, except for the benevolent assistance of good Samaritans in the community who kindly take them in. On visits to the ranch, my daughters and their cousins had nurtured and bottle-fed Timothy often when he was too feeble to have survived on his own.

Now, without any warning, my daughters realized that it was Timothy, their pet, being served to them in a sacrificial thicket of gravy. No angels of God to stop the hand of the carving knife. No ram in the thicket.

Perhaps ignorance isn't bliss. Perhaps living is something that must be done with our eyes open. And perhaps with some truth in our labels, we can choose to 'pass over' and cut out of our diets the gross injustices of life. Pass over, by not choosing. Save the bloody doorpost for the part of the story where I actually remember the atrocities that happened in the story to innocent Egyptian baby boys in the name of a bloody Passover.

I believe that "Pro-life" humanity has "God-given" the right to individuals to propagate our top-of-the-food-chain species and to have seeming *indifference* to our wake of voracious consumerism that follows close behind us. Spending billions to guarantee our 'rightful' place in nature. Blatantly replacing nature. Subtly replacing ourselves. The 'rightful' place of natural disasters guarantees our delicate and precarious place among **all** life.

Perhaps all life could live in balance without just human life assigning to itself extra degrees of specialness. Yeah, extra specialness just because the 'gods-who-made-everything' made us in their image, and we happen to have their same toes, fingers, and opposing thumbs. A Play-Doh miracle!! Really?
Doesn't it make more sense that humans invented these imaginary gods ...and hey, what a coincidence!!! ....They look just like us!

Perhaps there is a solution of "Pro-choice" living, minus any made up 'god given' rights, minus our 'living with eyes closed,' minus our minions of 'absolute' dominion, minus our playing to win. Win the egotistical implanted booby prize. Pro-choice minus the minions of corporate educators chanting, "win, win, win." Pro-choice in the name of responsibly and thoughtfully planned environments. Playing instead, not to lose. The exact antithesis of our socio-economic gluttony. Pro-choice in the form of noticing the impact of our sprawling cities and overgrown greed. Pro-choice by noticing that we are saving mankind at the expense of the whole rest of nature. Life-supporting machines stuck into the noses, arms and hearts of our absolute, supreme holy beings (well, at least the special ones who can afford it).

Oh yeah, save the whales? How about disconnecting a human? Disconnect our sprawling greed, bullying, and short-sightedness. Excuse me for my diversion. I wrinkle at the things this pen allows me to write. I'm obviously shedding some skin. Dangling by my heels. Exploding from the sting of SLAP on my inner child ass, and waaaaa coming out as my literary scream.

13

Death, birth, resurrection. And an assault rifle.

The unexpected knocking at the door scheduled itself into my Christmas day. What to my wondrous eyes should I see? Paul, whom I had met many years ago when I was studying the experiential, transformational EST-like workshops. He looked like Machine Gun Kelly. Holding in his arms a gift. Wrapped like a semi-automatic assault rifle, pretending to be a gift.

This was Christmas day. Ten o'clock. I'm with my relatives. The afterglow of St. Nick's visit still lingering like a yawn about to exhale. The smell of new pajamas, synthetic plastics and shredded packaging giving way to the aroma of butter, skillets, and Swedish pancakes in the kitchen.

Somewhere, not so far across town, there must have been a mother, her children, and similar aromas wafting through their house. Excusing the absence of their dad, Paul at ten in the morning. My id deployed its instinctive appetite for survival, interpreting millions of synaptic bits of information as I received my guest. Detecting pheromones, visual and auditory signals, a posture, eye, head and hand movements. Like an oceanic trawler sonically searching the sea bottom for sunken treasure. Was there a doubloon hidden in the erection of his surprise early morning visit?

Having given up hunting as well as having given up my 'last days' millennial survivalism, I received his cryptically gracious gift, knowing that it wouldn't be used for either. Attempting to be a gracious receiver, I unwrapped the Mack 90 assault rifle and its accompanying banana clip as if it were a fine bottle of wine.

The usual 'oohs and aahs' and 'how thoughtfuls' found their shallow place among his equally shallow respect for my cousin Greg. Hiding behind his generosity to me was his banana clip bone for Greg's wife. The note read, "Don't tell Emily." I tucked it back in the box as I recalled the words of Lennon, "Happiness is a warm gun." The gun was his way of subtly inviting my cousin Greg and his wife to his next transformational workshop retreat. The "Don't tell Emily" part was his way of trying to keep from his wife Emily his intentions for Greg's wife. The transformational trainings only served as his ticket into the swamp of oneness goo where he could overshadow the Marys in his life. Not unlike his biblical examples of Abraham, Isaac, Jacob, David, Solomon, and God 'the highest' before him. All using the stupefying powers and non-sense of the transcendental experience to selectively lobotomize their way to a woman's heart.

●●●

I was being cynical when I said earlier in my story that I couldn't tell you what goes on in transformational trainings till four in the morning. I spent many hours attending and later staffing these types of trainings in the early nineties. These were often multiple-day events that sometimes lasted till the early hours of the morning. Sleep deprivation works well in transformational trainings. It was in these workshops that I began to understand my confusion with the new-age message of unconditional love.

How do open, trusting, unconditionally loving friends intermingle with any degree of predictability? Does trust, plus forgiveness, divided by self-respect, equals the square root of unconditional love? Having just learned in these workshops to be unattached, and to claim my power, I soon realized how I had just traded one religion for another.

Pretending at truth in the name of my inner child.

The transformational workshop experience, like religion, selectively lobotomizes reality into gangs of adult 'inner children.' There are always the enticing short-term benefits and results of unconditional love, or group oneness. But adults will always be selfish individuals. Soon, organizing any group oneness and equality into leaders, followers and 'special' people. Adults know too much to pull off innocence minus their own libidinous predilections for any length of time.

●●●

Brad called to tell me that our friend Dave had been burned in an explosion. "…Over ninety-five percent of his body." God, it was awful. It happened so unexpectedly that it jolted all of us. Us means a group of my friends that I came to know at the dawn of my new age. It eventually included dozens of people. But Dave was there in the beginning of my trip down the yellow brick road. "Ninety-five percent?" I pictured red skin in my mind. His eyelashes gone. Maybe blisters that would delay our plans to mountain bike

the White Rim Trail in the Four Corners area of the desert southwest.
Easter. Eggs. Spring. Life.

But the gravity of Brad's voice suggested this information was the real thing. None of the usual 'attachments." Brad usually called to invite himself to my parties or gatherings.

>Attachment. Left click. "…I really want to bang on your wife."
>Back. Full screen. "I really value your friendship."
>Attachment. Left click. "I'll get you wasted, then bang on your friends' wives too."
>Back. Full screen.

"….He's been life-flighted to the burn unit at the University hospital. He has third-degree burns over ninety-five percent of his body."

(long pause) "He needs our energy and prayers."
(Longer pause) "Thank you for calling me Brad."
(click. silence.)

I didn't want to accept the reality of the phone call. I wanted my visit to the burn unit to be different. I expected bad. Skin grafts. Therapy. It was much worse than that. By the time I made it to the hospital, Dave was swollen so badly over his entire body that the shock had thrown him into a coma. There was an air of inevitability. Dave had always been the first of my friends to dive right into my mystical travel adventures in the desert. He was the classic neophyte. The fool. Pressing the envelope of conventions in life. He left behind three daughters, his ex-wife Katie, and his girlfriend lover of five years, Shelly.

I sensed that Dave's situation was far worse than bad. The literal hell that he would go through surgically, physically, and socially, was inconceivable. His last words as he fell out of the front door of the burning building into the arms of his co-worker were, "I'm going to make it through this." We all wanted that to be true. I left the hospital that night, knowing that it was not.

Just the week before, I was invited to dinner with Dave and Shelly and had to turn down the invitation. I was also going to have to turn down his invitation to go camping in the desert that weekend. And I had not called to tell him yet. Procrastination took care of things for me. Eventuality has a way of doing that.

I began my process of mourning early. They unplugged his massively swollen and oozing body two days later. It was a freakish, beautiful thing. The beauty came out only as I tried my best to rationalize the 'perfection' of his absence. I was told at his viewing by a close friend that Dave had made arrangements to meet with a 'shaman' to be administered a certain South American herbal tea called ayahuasca on the day of his accident.

This tea is sometimes nicknamed the 'death drug' for how effectively one leaves their body during the experience. It is not unlike its pharmaceutical equivalent, DMT, short for:

thebestfuckinghallucinationknowntomankind

It feels like getting shot out of the barrel of a high-powered rifle, with eyes like a fly, surrounded by a panoramic Mandelbrot set, a geometric flowering, like cherry blossoms in Springtime on seventy-eight speed. All packed into one Pythagorean synapse. The omniscience of a god, unleashed into a cosmic mobius of matter and sensual knowledge. Death, birth, resurrection, cosmic connection and a universal love that feels like a heart orgasm. All this and more, but Dave got mortally burned and dosed up with painkillers instead. Different shaman, same path.

I'll remember him for many things. Like when he would heckle his Sunday school instructors over points of understanding. His points of understanding me. His latitude over his longitude that included everyone in his unique way. With a wink. An impromptu visit, or phone call to just say Hi. His loyalty when my decisions were tipping the dominoes of my structured world. His respect for things greater than ourselves. Respecting his self, greater than any other thing. For that, I thank him. He was also reckless, unconventional and immature. He, too, came with his attachments.

I met him years ago, pre-fire, pre-workshop, pre-new age. Devout Christians. Curious cats. Unwinding the yarn ball of the mysterious Christ. Layer by layer, unwinding the *absolute* rightness of those who have tried to own the miraculous powers of our holy selves. Priests, parents, tithe collectors. I remember once the Sunday bible class instructor saying, "Anyone may answer this question but you, Dave." Selective reasoning, at its best, is found under the roof of religion. But, then again, so is pure faith. Sheep know their master's call. Whether they be the ninety-nine in the herd, or the one sheep straying. I've been both. Wandering the hills of holy lands in my head, looking for clues. Answers.

I'm Capricorn, remember? I have an appetite for esoterica and history. I love reading books. Hundreds of them. Philosophy, psychology, Egyptian, Sumerian, and early Christian texts. Remembering back, I clearly recall how I unraveled religion from my mentalisms. Having set my hand to the literary plow, I did not look back. And book after book I discovered the nakedness of my god. The mystery of 'his' godliness. The apple tasted good, and I did eat. How can I go back on that? Wring myself out?

•••

Less than two years after Paul's Christmas day visit, he stopped by again to fill me in on the details of his imminent sentencing. Oh, I haven't told you yet. I was watching the news one day and was baited with a teaser about a big ecstasy drug bust out at the international airport.

Ending a five-month sting operation, DEA and FBI operatives had closed in on Paul. Arresting their subject and an unnamed female passenger with an undisclosed amount of ecstasy in his car and an AK-47 in his trunk. Holy shit! I watched in surprise and amazement.

Surprise that, here was my friend Paul in a drug bust. Amazement that barely one year ago, Paul and his wife Emily were still teaching bible study classes, at their pastor's request, to inmates at the prison.

Amazed, because I had believed that his intense personality had only been coupled with a zealous commitment to his religion. He was basically Mr. Clean, barely a divorce and a dozen months earlier.

I felt anger at a system that deifies, yes, that deifies guilt and punishment and parades it in front of a sensationalized Heil, *Heil, Heil* shouting populace.

War! War! War on drugs. Hang for us the mascot Mussolini offender so that we may get our hit.

And they cry, 'crucify him.' And he was. And they roll over and have a smoke.

I wanted to disbelieve the stories they painted about Paul. A cache of weapons…, a drug ring…, a king pin…. O.K., the guns should not have been in his trunk, but he was only being vigilant. Readying his lamp with oil so that if his bridegroom Jesus happened to arrive as a thief in the night, he would be there ready to snip the ears off Roman soldiers. Ready to protect his Lord. Defend the faithfuls. The guns were his teddy-bear stash of unleavened bread lest his master's call be heard announcing Armageddon. But his flagrant Dangerfield recklessness had caught up with him.

News traveled fast. Even amongst friends. Especially amongst friends. We took a long drag of the sensationalism, got out hit, and lit the phone lines on fire. Have you heard? Watson, Watson, are you there? And the cock crowed once.

Natalie, have you heard the news? We called her in Los Angeles, but having been a producer for our local investigative channel three news team, she already had three versions of the story. A close friend of Paul's, Natalie had been in that very car one week earlier when she was in town visiting. That same car! With AK-47s in the trunk! It could have been her, instead of Paul's girlfriend, innocently strung up with the Mussolini. The gossip thickened. And the cock crowed twice.

By ten o'clock that evening, all his faithful friends were thirsty for the latest spin from the second round of investigative news.

Connecting the now 'large stash of guns' to the knock at the door, Christmas day, and the gift he had given me years earlier, I couldn't help but think about his first puff of the magic dragon. I was there to watch him do it. This was back in the days when experimental substances were letting me into heaven through the bathroom window on a regular basis. I thought it would last forever. And that it would be harmless… But it wasn't. And the cock crowed thrice.

He finished his detailed festival of what had led up to his being busted. Then he summed it up with his current psychology of life…All is nothing; nothing is everything. For a man about to be patted down, stripped, and cavity searched for remnants of anything personal, he seemed passionately assured, like my new ager friends, that everything is nothing. Just a thought. Of course, for the moment he still had his new woman, his new car, his business, his weekends with his children, his private lifestyle.

I see his commitment to his proclaimed nihilism as being much like my voice of anti-crony-capitalism and anti-commercialism. Condemning the very towers that I have my ladder leaning against. Condemning from the safety of my car, my house, my job, my creature comforts and supermarket living. But I've seen towers crumble and ladders fall. So, in that sense, I understand Paul. Everything, from a particular point of view, can quickly be reduced to nothing. And from seeming molehills, I've watched mountains form. So perhaps I, too, am a nihilist. As would be God, if he existed. Where else did "formless" and "void" come from if he did not create them first? The destroyer god, playing with creation.

•••

What we filter through our experiences, becomes our knowledge. And knowledge, according to Webster, is simply just that.

"That which is or may be known."

So, knowledge is what I am left over with, but, it may also often be at odds with, the actual experience. True, "everything is just a thought," as my New Ager friends say. But watching my daughters ride a bike for their very first time. THAT was everything. Watching them learn to skate and enjoy the outdoors was everything. All else was nothing. "Live for today" is the song of the damned in the bible. Yet that is the nature of my humanity. I am having my real human experience first, then I proceed to have my thoughts about it.

My life can only be lived right here, right now. Not back then, over there, or in a belief for the future. The notion that everything is just a thought has everything to do with degrees of relativity. Relativity to where I am in that moment. Cold to me might be warm to someone else. Everything seems to depend on relativity.

What if two, plus two, plus two, is quantumly heavier than three plus three?

When everything in the world gets reduced to just a thought, or nothing, as my new ager friends and nihilists proclaim, then senselessness starts throwing metal chairs at Chevy vans and adding sand to drinking water. And that is because the current moment begins to matter less than a future moment. The notion that 'everything is just a thought' does not explain how I felt when I held my baby daughters for the first time. Perhaps everything is matter, and my egotistical human mind then has thoughts about what matters most. Some human minds, however, cannot resist the notion that a human mind must come first, and then have the thoughts by which matter acts. Soon these thoughts are credited to gods, and then religions are created thereafter so that someone else can make sense of those thoughts for them.

●●●

I've heard recordings of sounds made by whales as they travel under the Polar icecap. It sounds beautifully haunting. My *self,* when it feels like I am leaving my body through focused meditation, also makes little noises like pings, tings and pops in my head. They sizzle, fizz and echo as my skull cavity seems to become the size of space itself. The noises resemble those of whales speaking. My body, at those times, *feels* like nothing. Sometimes, it feels like I leave my body.

I haven't figured out exactly where, who, or what 'I' is when 'I' is outside of my body. 'I' tells myself that 'I' is everything. In everything. Novelty and comprehension at the same time. The opposite of specific. A seeming point of viewing everything from what is best described as 'I's a little black box. A 'something' or an 'I' that is recording everything. Capturing all it does with seeming indifference to 'I's' sensing body.

True poppy field mathematics here. It will make 'sense' later. 'I' always comes down, back, whatever. Although for a while, 'I' continues to feel like 'I' is everything. In everything. Like a god, only better, because it's me. That's when 'I' does weird things. Like, talk about the oneness, free love and other beatitudes. 'I' loses the idea of urgency, and time may even dissipate. There is no getting to the "was it good for you?" scene because there seems to be no end. Again, no specificity. But out-of-body experiences, beliefs, good orgasms, being high, tripping and meditating, all come to an end.

When I is eventually me again, and my sensing body is all that is, 'we' (me, myself, and I) comprehend the thin layer between everything and nothing. Being and nothingness. Reality and eventuality. I am first human, being a nihilist. I am, therefore, a humanist nihilist. So, I can never really comprehend the concept of absolute nothing. Perhaps everything is everything, and nothing is nothing, and I am the space in-between. The point of view.
The human, being.

•••

So here I am writing about MY out-of-body experiences. CAPITALIST! I, too, have my own white light experience to share, dredged up out of the early nineties. Why I make it O.K. for me and less O.K. for all the others competing for my shelf space is that I don't give a shit about recruiting followers. I don't give a god damn if you believe my stories or not. I'm not outwardly peddling Jesus, oneness or how to ascend with my right hand, while, in secret, money changing with my left. I openly want you to descend into your wallet and buy copies of this book for your friends. I want my story, to be face out on the shelf. Gainfully employed profiling me as a publican. A fat camel. Knees unbent before the eye of the needle. If that offends you, stop reading.

My story is what happened from my perspective. I never meant to write it. I thought it was bizarre, scary, and entertaining when it happened. You may think that I am spreading the details too thin, tearing the wonder bread of your expectations. I want to spread the legs of my story for you properly though. Make sure that I get all the edges.
You've had the all-beef-patty-melt that was mostly bun. The tantalizing picture in the

menu oozing with lettuce, pickles, tomato, and drenched with sauce. When you order from the menu, you *expect* repetition. You want each bite to look like the advertisement. Sauce out to the edges. This was the nineties, after all. Safe sex redefining summers of love. Unprotected anything was only spreading dis-ease.

So, I'm using 'condiments' in my story. 99% effective if read completely before the climax. Useless if all you want is the beef patty. A fast-food quickie. And you wouldn't respect me in the morning anyway. So, I'll continue to fill you in on some details. Serve from the left. Clear from the right. I will come back to **my** "white light" experience. And yes, I'll get to the part about being naked in the desert, choking Rob, and to the gun in the hallway.

14

The first real space cowboys.
Or, turning vegetation into jubilation.

It all began on the sixth floor of the Belvedere. This was after the sleep-depraved years of transformational trainings, but before the sleep-depraved years of transformational drugs. Daniel had invited me to join him for a late summer evening dinner. Daniel was always good for some haute intellectualism. Or perhaps the latest spin on some new secret health diet regime, or esoteric movement.

I met him at a discourse on Odin and Votan years earlier. I liked his interest in studies of health, hallucination, and food sciences. He was also willing to humanize the Jesus of the bible and naturalize the concept of a supernatural god, which made conversation easy. I knew the evening would be full of boundless and rational exploration of current ideology.

Passing through downtown on the way to a popular outdoor restaurant, Daniel asked out of the blue,

> "How about stopping by my apartment to take a little puff of marijuana?"

The generation gap that separated Daniel from using the current street slang also insulated me from recoiling at less acceptable terms like smoking weed, grass, pot, or a drug. His invitation slipped under the covers of my moral rectitude. I had not been invited to do 'marijuana' since I was in high school when I had obediently refused it.

> "O.K," I said.

The words were out of my mouth before I could say,

> "Get thee behind me Satan."

Then I paused. Disbelieving my response, but doing absolutely nothing to change it.

•••

I recall the intrigue I had with the hippies in northern California when I was growing up. On Sunday afternoon, drives through Golden Gate Park, and in the streets of San Francisco. The ones I saw get busted outside of their van. I also had an adoration for my older sister, who was the Aphrodite of hippies. She was beautiful and independent, and made her own choices. At sixteen, she was running away from home. Hitching boxcar trains back to Chico, alone. She was totally immersed in the late sixties liberated counter-culture. I idolized her freedom. My mother didn't.

Once, I recall my mother hung on the wall a poster that had pictures of all the known street drugs. Dope, heroin, amphetamines, barbiturates, cute little yellow jackets, uppers and downers. This was her attempt at having the rest of us conform to be her Orwellian spies. To abuse our own nature and sniff out the non-prescribed, socially unaccepted drugs that my sister was using to slip free from conventions. I was mesmerized by the poster.

I remember reading and re-reading the desired effects each pill would supposedly have on the user. The equally supposed adverse effects. The plethora of nicknames for each pill. Learning the difference between a 'lid' and a 'lude.' Perhaps the poster helped create the very thing my mother feared when she brought it home to hang on the wall…a loss of my being controlled… ten years later.

•••

Although raised a devout Christian, undefiled by drugs or alcohol, I still managed to roll the best pencil-shaving-filled joints in my high school biology class. Next to me sat my friend Craig, who successfully planted pot seeds in each of the plant aquariums scattered throughout the room. Even when he got caught, I was too safely insulated from 'evil' to associate my faux joints with the reality of being expelled. It was always just a game for me. Smoking, drinking, doping, sexing, these things were so far on the left hand of my god that they were like the shrunken heads of my anthropological small-town conformity. A mythological and categorical taboo.

Perhaps that is what felt so sexy about saying, "Fuck" for the first time in my life. I was sixteen years old. A sophomore in high school. It was like breaking the hymen of my oral prowess. The sound barrier of my free speech. I was suspended in the weightless and meaningless tingle of the afterglow that followed. By the time I had come down from my vainglorious moment, the arms of my guilt were waiting to receive me. The god I had sworn allegiance to was whispering into my ear the address of the nearest priest and confessional.

CHOKING GOD

While I was working on my tongue, my mother was working on my vinyl record collection, extracting every vile word from proximity to my listening ears. I came home from school one day to see, out of the corner of my eye, our metal trash cans filled with my record albums. She had 'placed a hot coal' in the lyrical mouth of every performer. Including my Leo Kotke albums. Which was ironic since none of his albums had any vocals accompanying his excellent guitar riffs. But he was guilty by association just the same. My mom uncovered his nakedness in the title of one of his numbers called "Vaseline Machine Gun." A piece he had indelibly christened after waking up naked on the beach in the middle of a volleyball game. Yes, he too felt the heavy hand of the inquisitor as she shredded his album cover with the same zeal that was given to Elton John's Captain Fantastical Larry Flintish cover as it bit the dust.

This experience came as no surprise. The volume of my musical appreciation had been hazed into silence in my youth by an unspoken code of reverence that ceaselessly permeated through our home. I remember in my junior high years, shutting myself in my basement room at night and putting a record on the turntable to fall asleep to. Don't ask how, but my mom could somehow hear through the floor the single decibel music and she would stomp her disapproval on the floor above me. I soon took the advice of the late-night DJ's and literally just,

"put the needle on the record."

Positioning the turntable next to my bed, I would fall asleep to the sound of just the needle on the record. No volume, pre-headphones, and spin the vinyl grooves into my uncensored consciousness.

•••

It is easy for me to look back and be cynical about these events in my life. However, at that time, I was tolerant of my parents' shepherding. Molded by their parents, who were molded by their parents and their parents, they were products of the new age of religious revivalism that has scorched America with its post-French revolutionary spiritualism and Pentecostal fury.

Family bible study began promptly at six a.m. And if the previous evening's angelic succubus visits had found favor in me, I would often be startled awake with a glorious morning erection.

"On the count of three…,"

My mother's bible study wake-up call would demand that my feet be on the floor before she left my room. This was usually O.K. if my erection was the normal sleep-induced male behavioral kind. These would vanish in a moment before she got to "three." It was the all too frequent pee boner that slated me for insurrection. It had a mind of its own…
The more that she demanded that I,

"Awake and arise",

the deeper and harder it dug in its heels. Defying gravity.

Perhaps my subconscious mind was also digging in its heels, hoping for a moment's reprieve from biblical sanitation. But there was no time to lose. Jesus was coming soon for sure, and my mind had been seduced into thinking that I would be caressing his wounds with my tears in a kingdom of God with my family.
My family, that is, without my sister. While we were watching news clips of Patricia Hearst waving handguns at bank tellers side

by side with her alleged kidnappers on our thirteen-inch black and white, my sister had taken to the long and winding road again.

Leaving behind only a brief note, she had run away from home for the second or third time. Months went by, and we didn't know if she was dead or alive. Hopping trains to nowhere. It seemed like my mother was always praying, fasting or crying for her. My mind was too sedated by my beliefs to know that I had similar wings. Let alone that I, too, could leave the nest or fly the coop. I could only wonder dumbfoundedly at Melissa's way of life that paid no penance to unseen gods.

Following a tip from a postmarked letter we received from her after ten months of complete silence, my father flew to Mexico and met with a local clergyman who directed him to the district of the postmark. Passing from town to town, he miraculously found her in a small town, living with her communal friends. No running water. Love and oneness oozing.
I can only imagine what that reunion looked like. The version I got was somewhat akin to the "certain father" who killed the fatted calf for his prodigal son, …minus the fatted calf. Whatever the enticements, she embraced his

invitation to come home, only to leave again as soon as she turned eighteen.

She was the Martin Luther of our family. Nailing her statement of emancipation to the door of convention, she turned into the wind and left behind for good the religious shepherding of our parents and forefathers. She was the first real space cowboy. Pre Neil Armstrong. One small step for her siblings to follow, one giant leap for our budding consciousness.

•••

The adverse effects listed on the poster my mother hung that day did not seem all that adverse. At least not in the way I noticed my sister embody them. Mellowed down and groovy. Some part of me could see through the dark glass of conformity, and I would dream of things she was doing or places she had been. Nevertheless, our family was still hell-bent on being heaven-bound. Taught to anticipate with every passing day the proximity to our god's second coming.

It is for this anxiousness, this religious zealousness, that I dedicate this next poem. I wrote it to express my perturbation with some authors I was dealing with who needed distribution for their self-published novels.

Circa the mid nineties, I was working at a young local publishing company in a predominantly religious region of the country. A good amount of time was spent reviewing books sent to us by various authors. Naturally, a predominant portion of them had a religious slant. I often found myself swimming in piles of Christian hullabaloo as each writer sought to capitalize on the coming new millennium. Which meant to them a thousand years of peace. Which naturally turned into more big-brotherly judgment as each one sized up the next for their rightful piece of the capitalistic Christian literary pie.

Clothing their God's pierced body with a little spiritualistic profiteering. And often condemning bookstores and publishers for the lack of sales for their mostly unoriginal banter. Wearing righteousness on their sleeves, and money where their mouth was. Wanting to be humble and pretentious at the same time. To drive and look backwards at the same time. Like those cars on the freeway that are out of alignment and look like their tail end is traveling in a different direction than their front end.

Ambitious followers. Following out-of-touch leaders. Usually a combination of both. And figuring it all out literally kept these authors occupied. Fiction at its best. Armed with the typical slash-and-burn method of placing motes in their neighbor's eyes and overlooking the beams in their own. Their books did a better job filling garages and storage units instead of bookstores and literary clubs. It can often be difficult to be true to a cause or a message when money gets involved.

Morally correct causes fail because of eyesight problems. Losing focus. Selling abstinence from money or the amoral left, while at the same time being obsessed with both. So here is my apocalyptic ode to the rhetoric of causes and believers in life.

And in that day
Riders black
With stallions fierce
Pierce apocalyptic nipples
Erect with illusory
Messianic milk
That suckle pressing lips
And gnawing gums
Soothing knots of fear
And pangs of 'Confucian'

RICHARD CARLSTON

From 'Simon says'
Maniacal
Religious confusion
That burns the books
Of the fatness of life
Behind holy doors
Of holy wars
Of godless politicking
Grand peeping Thomas inquisitors
Adorned with compass
And squares and
Architecturally correct pews
Of congregate fortunates
Obla-ting the oh-blah-dahs
Of pentecosts
And baruch atah's
That line the pockets
And the seams
Of holy veils
And holy grails
With penitent graces
And tear swollen faces
And all the while
Some know and some don't
Some believe
And others won't
Just what it takes
To save mankind
From all the smokers,
Pokers, fags, hags,
Thieves, Jews, coloreds,

CHOKING GOD

Witches, bitches, gangs, snitches,
White fascist pigs,
Rapists, therapists,
Cheaters, wife-beaters
Poets, scientists, cops
Liars, friars, dope-heads
Pope-heads
Elections, confections,
And misled erections,
The dumb, the mute,
The fatally brute.
Too much, too little of
Praying, obeying,
Of sexing and laying,
Of treats, sweets,
Beers, queers, thugs, drugs,
And whatever "that" was,
Nudes, prudes, swearing and cussing,
Porn and corn-holing hedonists,
Masochists, chain-toting sodomists,
Leather clad masters and slavers,
Dictators, masturbators,
Health nuts, cheep sluts,
Gonorrhea, diarrhea,
Fen-fen, army men,
Motels, hotels,
Brothels, boils, spoils,
Disease, legal-ease,
Professions, confessions, sex shows,
And god only knows. God only knows,
But he's not tellin'

Who's free?
And who's the felon?
When the doors of heaven rise
Or whom the gates of hell surprise
So fatten up on life my friends
And button down the hatch
Take the scenery in
Work hard, play hard
Worry not if it rhymes
Or if it has good meter
For a pumpkin eater had a wife
But couldn't even keep her
And that's the way life is
It seems
It isn't what it ain't
We live until we don't
No different for a saint
So thank Charles Darwin
For random selection
And natural perfection
Is just what you are
So for Christ sake, Be perfect!
You see?
The words are what YOU make them
Not what they're said to be

●●●

So, I sat in silence in the back seat of Daniel's car. Doing nothing to change my O.K. to a no way as we made our way to his love shack at the Belvedere. This was no ordinary "tin roof rusted" shack. He had gone to great lengths to build it out with a sunken Jacuzzi, smoke machine, mirrored disco ball, an imitation Lawrence Welk bubble machine, an outstanding view of the city and an incredible sound system. Everything was set for me to 'make of the words what I wanted.' To discover my wings. To eat the forbidden fruit. And before I could smother my disobedience, Daniel was holding before my face a hand carved pipe.

With a 'flick of his Bic,' he pressed the apple to my mouth, and "I did eat."

Drawing the flame into the bowl, turning vegetation into jubilation, I took my first puff of the magic dragon. Finding it easier than I thought, I held my breath like an obedient pothead "should" and soon found myself on top of my bushel with my light 'so shining.'

My god, it was excellent! Out of what blue did this come from? I felt every note of the music, which up until then had behaved like most music does. Zeros and ones, exacted through silicon chips, received, equalized, boosted, turned up, given volume, until imitation voluptuousness spilled out of left and right speakers as "music" to my ears. As the ideas of time and relativity slipped furtively beneath the surface of my new reality, the music seemed to disobey mathematics and roll into my head like waves of a circular ocean. Sometimes crashing in frothy swimming bubbles. Other times, hanging, suspended, while I whirled and dervished around a singular note. Toppling waves with just the tip of my finger. I caught myself from slipping slowly off the sofa by leaning my head back against the rest.

Readjusting my equilibrium, I had the cognizance to take in each note and, at the same time, become aware of water that was drip, drip, dripping somewhere. My senses were extra. I felt tears welling up in my eyes and wondered how something so beautiful could come to me through a 'damned' thing like smoking. Smoking pot. A drug. Not through the bible, Jesus, prophets, saints or vigilant church going. Not gift-wrapped as recompense for duty, obedience or penitence. Call it a short cut. Call it a quick fix, or the easy road. Be jealous as hell of it. Illegalize it. Condemn it. But the nature of it will still be free and harmless. Abusive people abuse drugs. Addicts get addicted. Unhappy people have 'bad' trips.

●●●

Free and harmless?.... Exactly what 'absolute' fears. Hates. Can't control. 'Absolute' tears down the easy way. Like those who bitch and moan about how little you paid for your computer today, when they paid so much for theirs yesterday. I now empathized with the hippies who were cuffed outside their van when I was younger. 'Absolute' busted their ass without so much as a wink for the circumstances by which their lives were the product. Like the Brits who busted Gandhi for peacefully adjusting his own equilibrium. The war on drugs is truly a war on families and friends. I know pastors, counselors, teachers, painters, CEO's, mothers, children and fathers who are all 'users' of drugs. And yet we only label as addicts or abusers, those who are not using AMA-sanctioned drugs. While, on the other hand, we fail to label as 'abusers' those who are 'prescribed' prescriptions, and those who are given the get-out-of-jail-free card. Platinum, of course. Paid for by company insurance plans, lobbied-for by the same health industry that pushes a legalized, tablet-sized virility, to an already erect, AMA doped-up society.

Recommended:…Daily allowance.

And all this is easily confused with both government and religious sanctioning of pre and non 'scription' users of Prozac, Ritalin, Aspirin, Zanex, Codeine, caffeine, alcohol, Adderall, Valium, and too many headache and sleep-manipulating drugs to mention. Of course, all AMA approved for your well-being.

These 'legal substance' abusers I know are your sons and daughters, fathers, mothers, and bosses. While on the left-hand of these 'sanctioned' drug users, other non-sanctioned drug users are peacefully working out their own equilibrium without ever stepping foot into a pharmacy or drug store. So, before the dotted line is signed on the ballot to lock abusers and their dealers away, ask if we are not just selectively condemning the ones who don't have the money, nonsense, or futility to use 'sanctioned' drugs that grease the slimy pockets of the AMA and its lobbyists. Lobbyists who grease the slimy pockets of our local legislators and ecclesiastical gods. Before we rat on our neighbor or watch ratings-motivated investigative news reporters on TV exposing the rampant "illegal" drug use among our society's children, first look at the motes in our own eyes.

Does our "Just say no vote" have any relevance whatsoever to the millions of those who find peace, liberty or the pursuit of happiness in the equally abused prescription drugs? Who's bullshit mantras is society listening to?

A legislator legislating, or a preacher predicating laws of 'rightness,' does not give a shit about my ass being pressed up against a fence and all the empty sermon band-aids that I'm left with to make sense of it all.

Oh, but wait! Today's new haute philosophical vogue tells me that my society can't 'cause' something to me. They tell me that I am not a 'victim', and can't be a victim of my circumstances. This 'new age' of awareness tells me I choose my life. That on some level, 'I chose' to be rear-ended four weeks ago when a teenager totaled my car. Which would also mean that, on some level, I chose to be raped as a child?

15

'Sailing on that Silvery Mist.'
Copulating with my own vulnerability.

If it sounds like I am preaching again, maybe I am. I've been conditioned well to become the very God that I am choking. It must be my way of gaining control over the monsters in my life. You don't talk back, so by the default of your silence I get to be right. Not you specifically. I don't even know you.

I must mean the psycho-exnihlo-auto-holographically-suggested you that has existed since the big bang of my words.

The you that I picture agreeing with, and sometimes kicking against the pricks of my words.

The you that is as real to me as I ever made Moses, Jesus or God in heaven.

And they are 'real.' Trust me. I know. Remember, I met Jesus in my closet one night. So, I am a true believer. Why else would I be so intent on choking their beady little necks? I wrote earlier that you wouldn't believe me if I told you about it. That was presumptuous of me. I was just less gratuitous with my own vulnerability at that point in my story. Your belief or disbelief may have broken the mood. How do I know? Because you are still reading, aren't you?

Is the 'you' that I'm writing to, my own demon?

Laughing back at my timidity from the safety of his trick with mirrors. My captor. Promising me my freedom, in the name of love, only to tighten his grip on my confessions?

My pretentious cynicism has more than once tucked me safe in bed. Eyes closed tight to rejection. I blink, rub my eyes, and finger the golden bead of amber plucked from the clam of my tear ducts. Searching the nugget for inclusions of Pleistocene mania, I find no solace or answers in the tealeaves of my sleep jewels. My cynicism tells nothing and hides everything. Giving you, my reader, the proverbial name, rank and serial number of my captive story. I am the unsung hero of my own freedom. Pulling my fingernails out one by one. Torturing the weak spots. Looking for my true confession.

RICHARD CARLSTON

Toss the dripping coals aside
Blow off another page
Suck another spinner down
Exhale a lover's rage

Lovers. Ah yes, the lovers. I look up and notice over at the bar a young cupidic couple, legs intertwined, succumbing to the mating dance.

Her head tossed back as he dangles vinaigrette-chilled pasta above her swallowing hole. Her erect tongue reaching out for its limpness. Like a baby chic, submissively bobbing her head for the mother's succulent worm. They play with their food a bit. Then, get up and leave. Giggling on their way out. Abandoning the pasta.

Rage.
A lover's rage.
Is that the fire to my faggot?
Stuffed into the bellies of my emotions.
Into the belly of my Jesus.
Then into the bellies of my Gods.
Choking them all with my jealousy.
Ah yes, love.
The heartbeat of jealousy and all my emotions.
Love,

Stuffed into jealousy.
Stuffed into rage.
Rage at myself.
For copulating with my own vulnerability.
And feeling used afterwards.

●●●

My knee-jerk reaction has been to please others first and fake my own 'happygasm' later. You should know. I've been hoping to please you first with my spectacular vernacular while I eke out bits and pieces of my own rice water and cockroach story. I've learned to keep my secrets swallowed. But 'the days are accomplished that I should be delivered.' The transparency of my rage kicks and jabs from the swollen belly I've stuffed myself into. Head down. I've dilated my story to a three. Worth being admitted. Braxton Hicks giving way to rhythmic contractions.
Breathe, Rich, breathe. Hold. Push. Scream.

> Earth and sky
> And blown chaotic
> Nature
> Exercised
> Brought to bear
> Upon itself
> Intertwines

The serpent
The mother
Nature
Slithering
And misbehaving
Her directions
Her sturdy things
Rearranging
Understood things
And defying herself
The fool
Mother nature
And indifferent
And unrespited
Tears apart
Her holy places
Her sanctuaries
And then times of chaos
And surroundings
And being unusual
And cracking
At the seam of things
Boiling herself
And unrepented
Wets herself
Withers up
And bashes herself
At the hinges
Falls down
Rolls over
And smothers herself

CHOKING GOD

> …But for the lemon
> And puckering
> Stands up
> Inhales
> And spits out the seeds

Breathe again. I'm comfortably numbed now, and I'm going natural, so you'll have to put up with my unconventional unsedated writing style, which, as you've noticed by now, is punctuated to accommodate my stream of consciousness, not to sedate my thoughts into proper English.

I'm choking the English dog in me that used to sing, "love, love, love,… all we need is love." That mantra only works if we can get all the "broken-hearted people living in the world" to agree to let all their pains be. Only I've found that sermon to somehow work better on happy, well-off people. I'm happier when my pockets are filled with what my pastors called "the root of all evil." From that perspective it's easy to imagine the world living as one. No heaven, no religion,…"it's not hard to do." But how can we truly live as one with a demonstrably unnatural intention of everyone being equal?

> "The poor we will always have with us,"
>   as the Jesus so eloquently stated.

•••

The Belvedere had become the place for turning on, tuning in, and dropping out. It was our burning bush. Our Sinai. Our trips were always the fault of an invitation from our muse. Who or what she or he was to each of us, we never talked about. Yet there, standing at a gate, was our muse. Bidding us to 'Sail on a Silvery Mist.' We had no mentor. No opium den to wrap its loving arms of iniquity around us. No gateway drug instruction booklet to make it easy and child-safe. But it was always about the size.

We made up our own cue cards:

1. Get a bigger amount of whatever shit you took last time.
2. Get fucked up.
3. Wish you had taken more shit.
4. Make a mental note to get an even bigger amount of shit next time.

We measured everything. And our muse made sure that we followed instruction number four. Like Crick and Watson. Smashing our senses with what seemed would make a productive collision. Believing that we were ascending.

This one particular night, we had prepared a tea for the three of us by boiling almost an ounce of mushrooms. This would quite surely take us off the high dive. Our muse had been thorough. Using her best coy forty-five.

The Belvedere was not known for its cutlery or kitchenware. We finally found a suitable grail in the form of a glass blender into which we poured our tea to let it cool while sitting on the smooth marble counter like an Ark of the Covenant. We each 'reverently' placed our cups in front of us, and I reached to pour the tea.

This lesson in physics taught us two things. First, that a glass blender without its bottom screwed on, can still contain four cups of hot tea, if placed, just so, on a marble counter. Second, that it definitely is about size. Or at least quantity. I grabbed the handle of the blender, and as I raised it off of the marble, the tea sloshed out of the bottom, onto the table, and then onto the tile floor.

My heart sank. In those days, that amount of shrooms was hard to come by. We all took one look at each other, and, without any words, dropped to our hands and knees and started and started licking and slurping whatever tea we could off of the tile floor. Stopping. Wondering beyond all hope. Hoping with disbelief. We did find that size or amount was relative.

Thirty minutes later, I was swimming through the carpet as if it were a sea of kelp. Being and oneness obliterated. An orgasmic detritus of everything and nothingness. Of intercoursing. Of seriously Altered States, in a William Hurt sort of way. I had seen that movie in the 80's with my friends in Baker, California, right when it came out. It disturbed me then because I knew little about what was going on. It disturbed me now, because I *knew* what was going on. The fear of having undone my molecules from this entire earth was only interrupted by the voice in my head saying,

"Rule number four.
…I promise to remember rule number four next time."

•••

All I wanted when I was a kid were black zip-up Beatle boots, to let myself be, like everyone else was being. I sinned in my wishful thinking. My mother made it clear there would be no Beatle shoes in our house.

She would later in life tell my niece, when talking about following Jesus, that children need to be taught to follow Jesus from when they are young , otherwise they ask too many questions. Oh? How old is appropriate? Two or three? When they believe every myth or fable that comes from their parents' mouths?

I misunderstood how a pair of shoes could make me as supposedly 'bad' as the icons, or Hey Dashberrys, that popularized them. But then again, I now understand how each pair of shoes travels its own winding road. Perhaps zipping up shiny new Beatle shoes on my heaven-bound feet would have been laying up a carnal treasure here on earth.

Thank God for my mother; I now have a god or two to choke; speaking of which, I am now feeling vulnerable enough to tell you about the time I met my God. So, getting back to my closet, I'll tell you about my 'white light' experience with my Jesus.

•••

I had gone back to my bedroom on that particular evening to look for something warm to put on. I needed something warm because I was naked and wet. I was naked and wet because I had been standing outside in the warm summer's night rain. I was standing in the rain because I was tripping on some exceptional mushroom tea with my friend Quentin.

The rain was a splendid addition to an already 'out of body' emotion of feeling like a large eyeball. Seeing three hundred and sixty degrees. Seeing with the balls of my feet. With my fingertips. With the skin on my back. The hair on my head. Feeling conversed words and the thoughts that made them as if they were tangible objects. Like a pond, acted upon by thousands of ripples. And underneath and through it all, being the water. The elusive, yet momentarily attainable, 'oneness.' 'The All.' The same oneness that has been abused, controlled, manipulated. Tortured out of the mouths of witches, alchemists, the unfaithful, and replaced with the hot coal of conformity.

The 'one' satient herd frightened by the 'oneness' of the pond.

Unable to drink it all. Damn it all. Dredge it all. Package it up into neat little boxes and profiteer it. Prophet it. Pope it. Minister it. Dipping just the toe in and claiming it for Spain, for France, Allah, Buddha, Jehovah. Spoiling it with conquest-crazed madness for ownership. Stacking bibles, codes and commandments on its shores and placing grindstones on the necks of those who dare enter its waters above the knee.

So, I'm standing there. Wet. In the rain. Free. I decide to put on dry clothes and join Quentin inside. Finding my way to my bedroom closet, I began searching for something dry, and my forehead touched the end of a hanger. That's all the stimuli I needed. The next moment, my 'eyes' found my *self* underneath a large olive tree. Next to a meandering dirt road. Next to Jesus. And he was right there, in his robes, as real as my mind's eye could make him. My senses created for me the touch, smell and swelling heart of a warm embrace.

Now, what happened next was the accumulated effects of my years in seminary and mystery school studies. Standing there with a tingling sensation lingering on my forehead, I found myself arching backwards as my chest filled up with an orgasmic explosion of emotions and a feeling of being loved from all directions in the universe. It felt once again like the blossoming of cherry trees budding all at once. My arms fell backwards as if I were being lifted by my chest.

After what felt like a long time, I slowly began to bring my arms back up to me, sweeping my hands around in a large windmill arc until my thumbs ended up on my outstretched tongue. Wetting my thumbs, and beginning to stand more erect, I found myself standing again before 'Jesus.' Reaching forward with my arms, I held his face in my hands, and my wet thumbs covered his eyes. What I said non-verbally was,

"Thank you for causing me to see."

Then I felt another explosion of more love than I could bear, and my body arched back again to contain it all. My arms once more falling backwards. Again, after what seemed like a while, I began to stand erect, sweeping my arms forward. Once again, my fingers swept around and onto my outstretched tongue. As I continued standing erect, I again found myself standing in front of 'Jesus.' I reached forward, embracing his face. This time, my wetted index fingers pressed into his ears. The emotion I felt this time, and that I again said non-verbally, was,

"Thank you for causing me to hear."

Then I kissed him on the mouth. Wrapping my arms around the hanging clothes before me, I slid down his body and wept at his feet. Next to my shoes and sweaters. When I had recomposed myself, I rose on one knee to get up and felt the fulfillment of my own mind-controlled beliefs…. "every knee shall bow, and every tongue confess…" There I was, kneeling before 'Jesus.' The thought came to me,

> "I'm kneeling to get up,
> not kneeling to grovel in humility."

"Of course!!" My 'Jesus' had heard my thought, at the same time I had it, and he 'said,' or I thought him saying,

> "Yes, that's right."

With the help of the shirt tails in my closet, I pulled myself up. All of this seemed to take about thirty minutes. When he began walking away, I wasn't sure if I wanted him to leave, and I called out to him.

> "Hey Jesus."

…in a tone unusual to me. More like Fat Albert saying;

"Hey, hey, hey."

He turned, smiled back at me, then continued walking away.

"Heeeeey Jesus."

Two more times, I called out. Each time, he turned, smiled, then continued walking away. One last time, I called out,

"Heeeeey Jesus."

This time he continued walking away, but raised his hand as if to wave back and say,

"You're o.k., you're finished."

And just like that, my psyche released me from bondage to my god.

●●●

I remember once attending a large costume party with over several hundred people. On a large stage in the front of the dinner hall, a hypnotist had gathered his select participants from the audience. Talking them into his hypnotic mantra, he soon had the audience in awe as these ordinary people did the most unordinary things. Men searching each other's pants for their "lost penis." Crying on each other's shoulders when they found them.

A girl was convinced she was an interpreter on intergalactic space flights where she met with, spoke to, and interpreted for us the sexual ways and love-making customs on other planets. She literally 'spoke' several distinctly different languages of alien races. Blushing as she made body gestures that were totally different from our style of lovemaking.

She was next told (by the hypnotist who had now become a 'preacher') that she would now have 'some ailment' from which she would want to be healed. Immediately she began crying sadly about how big her butt was. "My butt, ….it's so big!" she spoke through tears. And, when he asked her directly if she had anything from which she would like to be 'healed.' she answered, "Yes."
He then placed his hand on her forehead, and she was 'healed' of her big butt. She was so excited. She cried some more, thanking him, then she threw her arms around him. For the next little while, she kept feeling her butt and saying, "My butt, it's so tight."

Her date was watching her from the audience. She would never in her 'right mind' have gone up onto that stage crying and feeling her butt in front of hundreds of people. But here is my point. Neither would I have had a thirty-minute conversation with Jesus, in my closet, staring at a hanger. I had told myself after seeing several of these hypnotic stage extravaganzas over the years that I would never willingly choose to get hypnotized and mentally anchored to make an ass of myself on stage.

And yet I never knew, until I 'awoke' how completely I had given my mind to my Gods, and thirty-years later, I am still awakening. With the advantage of hindsight, I now see my tranced willingness to sell myself out to others 'counts of three.' To deep sleep-inducing lists of ten and Dudley-do-rightness.
A controlled egg becomes a chicken.

A controlled mind becomes aberrant behavior, cracking the shell of its own conformity.

● ● ●

As I stood in front of my closet reflecting on my visit with Jesus, I realized I was still naked, and I wanted to get warm. Putting on a sweatshirt that I had previously tried to throw away several times, I joined Quentin in the family room. He was curious to know where I had been for so long. I told him about the rain, my closet, and my visit with Jesus. Quentin was even more curious. "You mean you just now talked to Jesus?" Yes. "Well, I want to talk to him." He wanted to know if Jesus was still in my closet. Of course, I was still 'channeling' the after-glowing neuro-erotic presence of my heavenly, holographic God. So, I told him that I felt 'Jesus' was right there in the room with us. Quentin asked me if he could ask Jesus a question. I supposed so, and said, "yes." "How do I do it?" he asked. "Just start talking to him," I said.

Now, to put this whole scene into context, remember we had enhanced our evening with a cup of 'tea.' Steeped from the same family of fungus from upon which Mr. Caterpillar had asked Alice, "Who are you?" The same Amanita delicacy from which red-nosed reindeer derive their powers of flight. Or that fat, round little red and white metaphorical Santa's take to the sky bringing bounteous gifts to every single girl and boy. So, of course Jesus' presence in the room was as objectively real as the omnipresence of Santa. "I don't know how to talk with Jesus," Quentin said. "Can I just talk to you, and you ask him for me?" I supposed I could speak to Jesus for him, so I said, "yes."

Now, Quentin's life hadn't been going particularly well. He had been out of work, through a divorce, and he was living at his parents' home. His first question was to ask Jesus for a job and a place of his own again. My, I mean Jesus' response to him was, "Ask me for something I can give you." Quentin, puzzled, asked, "I want to find a woman who loves me." Again, the 'Jesus' in my head replied,

"Ask me for something I can give you."

To which Quentin then posited, "I just want you to love me." "Well, that I can give you abundantly," the Jesus replied.

"So, you mean I'm just fucked?"

"Yes." The Jesus replied. The answer was out of my mouth before I could think, 'sacrilege.' We both broke out in laughter at the preponderance of the whole conversation.

Knowing that we were just talking to each other. And yet, on a genuine level, we understood the basic truth of the foregoing drama. Asking any faith-created 'Jesus' or 'God' for a favor or a blessing is like asking my banker for a job, a house, or a lover. Not impossible, but improbable. With enough persistence, my banker might capitulate and hook me up with the job part. As far as a house, or something intangible like success, happiness, or better health… "I am just fucked," unless, of course, I promise some kind of security to the banker. Security that assures him a greater return than what he is giving me. If you follow the money, you'll usually see who is really receiving the favors. Contrary to popular evangelized opinion. The 'free-lunch' get-out-of-jail-free card usually gets dealt to the 'tithe collectors,' the ones who gainfully prey upon the faithful souls of the psychophants.

The tithe collector can be a god, a friend, a boss, a parent or a lover. You'll usually find them sitting behind the contract for contrition, benevolence, or a fat tithe. The participants in this game are labeled conveniently 'giver' and 'taker.' Insolated from others by their indifference, takers, like bankers, literally don't 'give' a shit. Neither do the iconic idols of fairytale beliefs, such as omnipotent gods. They don't 'give' anything. Perceived rewards are received for servile relationships. Again, just follow the money, or the servitude. So, I really am "just fucked" if I ask for the free lunch.

When I came to understand this principle, I became accountable and responsible for my life.

"If it is to be, it's up to me."

I also turned my whole world upside down. I was not used to giving my self credit or to thanking myself for saving my own ass. The credit for all the tight-spotted 'miracles' in my life had been given to my God.

How frustrating that must have been for my psyche, my id, that had been right there for me each time I 'asked god' and got something. My silent partner *self* that never got the credit for literally getting me to my new job, for avoiding that crash, for inspiring me to get off my ass and find ways to make my own house payment, to toil, like the lilies in Jerusalem.

I found myself having to re-define my great sell-out to my Gods and having to re-program my mind to accept responsibility for my own greatness. To forgive myself for my own mediocrity. My id had a hard time creating miracles or blessings for me because I was now taking the credit for my actions. This meant that if something was to be, it was really up to me. No more begging for blessings from an omnipotent, all-powerful, mythical god. During this time of my life, fewer miracles happened than ever before because I didn't know who to ask for them. Myself? Richard bless this, Richard bless that? I had been a perfectly functioning starry-eyed god machine. I used to expect miracles from my God and get them, sometimes. Now, I had become all short-circuited. There was no post-Christianity debriefing. No addiction rehab center where I could cope with my 'god' obsession and accept my own self-expression. Especially my miraculous self-expression.

Call it my id, my gut feelings, my premonition, my small voice in my head, my feelings that I follow. All these tools of mine are really pretty omnipotent when I stop to think how miraculous my being is. But I had been taught to be humble and selfless. And to feel guilty if I wasn't.

How was I to now take credit for and be responsible and accountable for all the events in my life? That proved to be easier said than done. Like the time I parted a storm while guiding a group of airline pilots up the Grand Teton in Wyoming.

16

Scouring the stick of life for one last everlasting tootsie savor.

It was precariously late in the fall of 1984. Much of the route we had chosen was covered in snow from a storm several days earlier. To top it off, a second storm was moving in from the west, undetected from our eastern approach. Our high base camp was positioned in the glacial moraine between the Middle Teton and the Grand Teton. The views from the camp are incredible. High above the tree line, the landscape is filled with huge rocks and boulders that have been dislodged over millennia from the rock faces above. Acting like monstrous bulldozers, glaciers have pushed up high mounds of rock and scree, dividing the moraine with tumulus walls of debris.

Climbers who plan to reach the high base camp early enough in the day get their choice of the best clearings in the boulders for their base camps. Water is usually gathered from little streams of melt-water on the glacier that form in the daytime and freeze at night. The whole moraine is shadowed by a ridge that runs north and south between the Middle and Grand Tetons. The sun sets early behind this ridge, leaving the moraine in an early darkness. We had retired early that night, planning to get up at three in the morning to begin our climb. The sounds of rock-fall ringing through the moraine played on our nerves like a grand orchestra, preventing us from getting any sleep.

At three AM sharp, we put on our headlamps, ate a quick breakfast, then began climbing up the face of the ridge. By five in the morning, we were standing on top of the ridge and could see east and west as far as the eye could see. In the early morning light we could now see the storm moving in fast from the west. Our group decision was to keep climbing, intending to reach the summit two-thousand feet above before the storm hit. Moving up the south ridge of the Grand Teton, we roped up and began the more difficult section of this ascent. Unfortunately, the storm moved faster than we had anticipated.

We had just finished traversing a ledge called Wall Street when the storm hit us. This ledge graciously starts out about thirty feet wide on one end and tapers down to nothing on the other. The exposure is dizzying. The climbing after that continued to get more difficult. First, a drizzle, then sleet, then ice, then snow slowed our advance. At first, it seemed only to add to our adventure. But conditions worsened quickly. Throwing caution to the wind, we kept ascending. By late morning, we had reached a ledge a thousand feet from the summit. Our ropes and water were frozen. One climber's toes were frost bitten. Visibility was near zero. The rock was now coated in a thick film of ice from the heavy sleet. We were in the worst spot on the mountain to try a descent in these conditions back down our ascent route. I decided to keep moving up. I knew of an easier escape route five hundred feet below the west side of the summit that would involve a critically negotiated traverse on ledges higher up. The traverse would position us above an overhanging cliff, below which was a thin ridge to the west and a steep scree-filled couloir that then led to the usual descent route off the backside of the mountain.

Finding the wrong escape route would put us in midair, literally. It would be critical to negotiate the traverse and end up exactly above the ridge to the West. All this in a complete white-out blizzard. The rock was now covered in ice crystals that made climbing nearly impossible. Cracks and fissures in the rock that were usually easy to insert climbing equipment into were now filled with ice. One particularly easy section to climb in fair weather called Friction Pitch, for its lack of hand holds, was now impossible to ascend. So, leading out around an arête, I found an alternate route made possible by a chimney crack wide enough to wedge my body into. Extra gear in my pack made it difficult to wedge, and then unwedge myself as I moved up, inch by inch. Reaching for an obvious outcrop above my head, my hand slipped off some ice, and the weight of my pack pulled me backwards.

I fell upside down and was caught by my last piece of protection, which stopped me abruptly. I found myself wedged upside down in the same chimney crack I had been climbing. My nerves were rattled. Adrenalin kicking into high gear, I quickly oriented myself and started over, this time making it past my high point. By climbing this route, I had bypassed the impossible ice-covered Friction Pitch section. I secured myself to a ledge above the others. At this point, I regretted my decision to leave behind in my car my rope ascending gear that was never necessary on this climb in fair weather. So, one by one, I had to pull each of the others up this section as they tried as best as they could to assist themselves.

Climbing in these conditions with four lives, for which I was responsible, was extreme. I only had one acceptable outcome - to get them safely off the mountain. Now, five-hundred feet and one lead-fall higher, we were in what I had figured to be the right altitude to begin the traverse to the west side of the mountain. The rock was now even more thickly covered in ice and sleet, and I had never actually needed to use this traverse route before. I only knew it existed. Incidentally, some climbers died exactly one year later on this same route, trying the same descent caught in similar conditions.

I needed some assurance that I could pull it off. All my skills and training left me facing the ferocity of Gaia with no one to turn to for help. So I'm just there, "fucked," as Quentin said earlier in my story. With my one acceptable outcome to contend with. Conditions were worsening. The four other climbers were relying on me to know what to do. We would freeze if we stayed where we were. Yet I couldn't traverse with them across the icy ledges unless I could get my bearings and see where we were going. I didn't want them to lose confidence. Demoralized climbers get sloppy, make mistakes and die.

So...I prayed. I prayed the mother of all prayers to my pre-annihilated God. I demanded a miracle. And it came. 'The parting of the storm.' Just like the Red Sea in Cecil B. DeMill's Ten Commandments. It lasted for only one split second. But in that one brief moment, I could make out the spot below us and to the west that we would need to reach in order to make our hanging-descent down the ropes to the ridge five-hundred feet below.

•••

Now tell me this. If there is no god, then to whom do I give the credit for this power over nature? At the time, I thanked *my* God. Over and over. But from my godless being now, I look back and only see my *self,* expressing. And my *self,* causing the results of MY petition. My holy self, expressing my miraculous, and getting us safely off the mountain. And it has taken me thirty years to give credit where credit is due.

...To undo my blasphemous 'thank god's'
and acknowledge my*self.*

Take pride in my talent, skill, level-headedness, determination, intuition and commitment. To accept that faith in my self, and the powers of my own vibratory petition, had split the ferocious thighs of Gaia's loins.

Oh yes, there is a God.

I believe it is my id. It is your id. Capable of being all-powerful. All-knowing. Yet unknowable. As I've come to know my 'self', as my own creator, as my own God, miracles are happening in my life again.
Like the mythical hero Moses, I remove my shoes from my feet and dance barefoot before my own magnificent burning bush of desires and willpower, obeying the commands of my own mouth and heart.

•••

Scouting our way across the ledges, we were enveloped in the storm. At the end of a blind descent down the iced-up ropes, I began swinging across the rocks to find a spot to anchor into for the rest to follow. I was completely unaware that the huge boulder I had secured the ropes to up above me was now loosening from the ledge with each of my swings back and forth. The others braced it and prevented disaster without me ever hearing their yells through the wind and snow. Rope length after rope length, we

eventually made our braille-like way to the point of no return.
The 'Rock of Gibraltar.'

One hundred sixty feet below its overhanging wall was the relative safety of the ridge below. The ridge led to a one-thousand-foot scree-filled gully and eventually to the warmth of our base camp below. The anchor point was well marked by dozens of nylon slings that had been left behind by others who had descended from this spot. We freed a few loops of sling from the ice, added one of our own, and rigged up our last free-hanging descent. One by one, we dropped over the edge like spiders and made it to tierra firma. Gary came last. The largest of us all. As he left the security of the rock above and began descending, the wind whipped him back and forth like a pendulum. When he came down far enough for us to see him through the storm, we noticed he was out of control. Tipping backwards under the weight of his pack, he was coming down too fast on the iced-up ropes. Racing to the bottom end of the ropes, we pulled them taught, slowing the ropes feed through his descending gear and controlling his descent.

Safely down, we negotiated the scree gully, sometimes locking arms to keep from being blown over in the wind. It was well after dark when we made it to our base camp. Expecting to collapse in the shelter of our tents, we instead found our tents had collapsed and the poles broken in the wind. Darrell and Steve's tent was completely gone, and their gear inside was scattered. Readjusting a makeshift base camp, we weathered the night.

On day three we hiked off the mountain with warm sunshine bathing our tormented bodies. The splitting of the storm was just a wink in time. I'm not saying I'm Moses or anything. But I do take credit for it. Would it have split anyway if I hadn't been there? I hate questions like that. That's perhaps why Moses just simply plagiarized his birth story from King Saragon's epic tale before him. And me, simply borrowing from Moses' story, the synchronicity of the storm's movement with my own?

....And the clouds split before me...

Just like my own basket of reeds, covered in pitch, floating me into the arms of a bathing beauty, conveniently waiting to save me.

●●●

God, I've been rambling for a while. The Teton story came from the thought of accepting my own self-expression, which came from the story of Quentin saying, "I'm just fucked." Which came from my white light visit with Jesus. Which came from the unordinary things that our minds create when we are mind-controlled or hypnotized. Which was a spin from my rage with love, gods, and my mother's God. Which was directly related to how 'real' I made these nether-land gods, and how real I've made the 'you' that I'm writing to. And that finally takes me back to the hippies, my mom's drug poster, my sister, my first toke of grass on the sixth floor of the Belvedere, what leaving my body is like, what whales sound like, and my style of nihilism. Tritely defined from my humanist point of view.

●●●

Yes, my religio-centrically engineered point of view. I wonder if humans would have the same "made-in-the-image-of-god" point of view if we actually knew the source of the fables that were the beginnings of our mythological Gods. If women and men could once again tear the hymen that veils the people from those priesthood types that designed those mythological gods. Would we continue to believe the stories of our tribal nomadic beginnings claiming that only our bi-pedal Gods, in the image of a man's likeness, created, named and have dominion over all things? We silly humans? Who destroy ourselves, in spite of ourselves?

When it all comes down to it, in spite of our human greatness, the earth will be around much longer than humans. Long after we've spoiled our mortal coil on this planet, nature, unabused by our myths, will still be around. In spite of our divined definitions and ego-centered name giving. Seems like the only thing that is *nothing* is our human thinking. Everything else is everything. Our fear of being nothing and our uniquely human fear of death have driven us into a frantic madness to control and hang onto everything. Name everything, define everything. How dare we humans, in our insecure madness, call anything in nature nothing, just a thought, or a creation of our Gods.! And when two planets collide on a summer's night or if a tree falls in the forest and I'm not there to see it, define it, name it, how dare I call that either nothing or God's omnipotence!
I am, and therefore, I am a human, being.

> The will, the mind, thoughts
> Are not matter, have no matter
> What's the matter, with that?
> Nothing!
> No thing, is
> What matter is, to most

Every*thing* matters, is matter. No *thing* is just a thought. I am just fucked if I expect something outside of myself to guarantee my place on this planet, whether it is a human-made God or a human-made constitution, promise, contract, friend or lover. Reality eventually reveals itself to me when I attempt to fake my human organism into perpetuity.

●●●

I know I seem judgmental, condescending and self-righteous at times. Perhaps all the time. That's my good old Christian conditioning.

> "Judge not"

….Yet in the same literally fucking breath I was taught to…,

> "Be not like the publicans"

> "Be not like the sinners."

So, in essence, to judge *everything!!*

Exactly like the publicans who give their alms openly, whose works we all certainly know.

...Have my eye fixed on heaven and *ascension* from this lowly earthly life.

So, in essence, con-*descend* everything else. Subtly, though, so as not to appear vain.
...Always measure whether I was doing too much of this, or too little of that. In essence, to be self-righteous. Right by my own mind's thinking.

So, I am repeating the same thing that I was taught to do so well.

My friend Harvey said that I tell you too often what a good Christian I was before I 'fell.' O.K., so I agree that I have braggard the Christian ass in me that I am now riding though the streets of my Jerusalem. I do it to thoroughly make clear to myself where the throne of my anger lies. Smothered in *my* obedience to, *my* beliefs in, *my* faith in, *my* love for, *my* style of, doing Christianity to myself.

It isn't the object of my desire, but the way I have desired that object that I am really choking.

Choking my unrealistic expectations that I placed upon myself and others. I was good, not as in good or bad. But good as in a big fat ripe cow, fully conditioned to be a fat ripe cow.

And back to the matter? Well, back then, I, like Rob, had convinced myself that nothing temporary mattered. I was living in a self-made bubble floating its way right up to heaven. However, my lollipop ship of goodness ascended too dangerously close to my belief-made God, undoing its sweetness to reveal my tootsie-roll center of all things. My new age.
But, like Icarus before them, my beliefs melted away before I could self-actualize them into reality. The chewy chocolate sacrament of my God, giving salivation to mastication, leaving only the mast of my expectations. Swelling one last time, then dissolving, my cravings unraveling and scouring the stick of life for one last everlasting tootsie savor. My Pinocchio nose that I had for mythical beliefs was swallowed whole by the Jonah whale of its exaggeration.

"Look over here,"

the holy trickster says.

"Don't notice the pink elephant."

"Your faith will save you."

But I was noticing pink elephants, and I was not saving myself with my faith.

17

"Eloi, Eloi, lama sabachthani?"

In the process of leaving the traditions of my religion, I had also denied my actual reality to the point of losing almost everything. Remember the ninety-seven percent gamble? The bad investment? The real loser? In the name of that faith and trust and positively affirmed attitude, I woke up one morning to find skid marks in the driveway where our luxury car had been the night before. Obviously, I had not yet developed the inertia of results-oriented trust in myself to replace the mass of inertia that faith in my Christian idealism had surrounded me with. It was like I had been given little commissary rations as 'Private Gentile' on my descent into reality.

My reasoning left-brain had dismantled the religious platitudes of my right brain. Such as hope for things not seen. My left brain has sought to preserve its structured leftness by sabotaging my unstructured rightness.

"It's not to get you to understand what I am saying," the left-brain says,
"It's to get you to understand, that what I am saying, is what must be understood."

The jealous stomach of the left-brain, like Dante's Inferno, consuming the paradise of my right brain.

●●●

The inferno of my reasoning has reduced many of my new-age friendships to ashes. Dante did a number on Paul's hedonistic paradise, pressing the sweet wine from the bitter skin. His prison commissary had this to issue him on entry to his Gulag, of course, after lifting his testicles and spreading his buttocks to search for contraband;

"…A red jumpsuit, white socks, tennis shoes, two flimsy worn sheets, a sheet-thin blanket, a cup, a plastic bag with a small toothbrush, toothpaste, Motel 6-sized bar of soap, a comb, a razor and a packet of shaving crème and I.D. badge."

His Golgothic cross?

And yet, from within the smoldering ashes of its reasoning and predictability, the uncreative left-brain cries out to the right,

"Eloi, Eloi, lama sabachthani?"

Which, being interpreted means,

"Right brain, save my ass."

And all of the pessimists said,

"Let us see whether Elias (the right brain) will come to save him."

The thing is, the right brain has no clue. Does not perform on demand. It just offers creativity and boundlessness. It doesn't know how to *save* the left-brain and bring conformity and rules into its right brain 'heaven.' So, the right brain creates a poppy field of illusion.

"So I'm just fucked?"

The left-brain sometimes asks. Of course, the right brain sometimes answers. What person, while in their left mind, wants to admit that the seat of our soul is a slug? A chemically proficient gland no bigger than a bean? An id. Genetically conditioned to hoard or search for satiety. The 'id God' who watches over all things, is literally in everything and in every thought I have, with a front-row seat to the battle of right and left. Caring little about petty losses, hurt feelings, shattered dreams,

broken commitments or who's right or wrong.
The little gland seems to care only about its own survival. For its one acceptable outcome, which is just to survive, gathering and adapting to information along the way. Protected deep within the thick armor of the skull. Every heartbeat, every movement is precisely executed to get it what it wants.

Satiety….and good drugs.

Yes, our little God gland is an addict of its self-produced equivalents for DMT, MDMA, LSD, THC and just about every other man-made or naturally found hallucinogen. Is the war on drugs a war on our 'God?' A war on our drug-addicted self? Our pineal ids?

•••

So here I am in the middle of a thorough word fuck. How serendipitous! Because at that time in my life, beginning at the Belvedere, I was skinny dipping in the oneness goo and word fuck of a new age god. Manifesting, meditating, breathing, speaking and eating my way into the kingdom of universal love and oneness. New shaman, same results as religion. Almost getting somewhere in a plethora of mind-teasing words, phrases and anecdotes that still left starving children in Africa and my bills to be paid. But I had the enlightenment bug, and this time, I really thought that I was on the true path to figuring it all out.

Never-minding the little habituated, subliminal Kilroy markings painted on every single new age fad or fixed belief that I embraced, I launched an all-out war against my entrenched conditioning. Feathering the troubled engines of my cosmic-oneness flying-fortress, I willfully delivered destruction on my past religious beliefs. Leveling the walls of Christianity and organized religions, I gloated at each direct hit. Ace of wands, king of swords, I was blind to the ripple effect this total deconstruction was to have on my life.

Who was this Kilroy that I had turned loose? I see a cartoon image of my id, a fleshy Mr. Magoo, deep within the windowless, Iron Mountain safety of my head cavity. Like the blind folded image of Justice, indifferent to the results of the scales in her hand, whitewashing Kilroy on each and every sentence she issued for each fixed belief in my life.

Funny, isn't it? That I would use Magoo to

describe my id. I remember him as a tiny little man with his eyes always shut. He was the opposite of Wile Coyote, who was always getting himself annihilated. Magoo's world, instead, rolled out a red carpet for him. If he was walking off the top floor of a skyscraper, a crane hoisting an I-beam would appear from the camera's left, and Magoo would blindly walk out into thin air only to be saved by the passing I-beam that would safely position him somewhere else. And off he would go, mumbling to himself as he continued his blind walk-about.

How was I to reopen my eyes, while my third eye was happily painting Kilroy on each fixed belief? Construction and deconstruction needed clear instructions. But from whom? My left, or my right brain? That battlefield will always remain bloody, with only brief moments of armistice.

•••

I found the answer through experience. Through a period of my life that I have labeled as 'The Visitors.' People started just showing up at my door. This would happen at all hours of the day or night. Each would bring with him or her their little bag of characters and stories. Some were wizards, some were jokers, some necromancers, others spiritualists, deceivers, connivers, alchemists, potion makers, deviants, devils, angels, givers, takers, friends, enemies, basically most every aspect described in the major arcana of the tarot. It was like watching an elegantly costumed and performed Broadway play. Complete with a playbill and cast of characters. Each visitor had a lasting effect on me.

I began to develop, out of the chaos, what Rupert Sheldrake describes as a "morphic resonance." A certain character set of personalities that seemed to be subject to definition. A morphing, changing definition, but nonetheless a pattern of discernable resonance that described a relationship between thoughts, ideas, people and events. It was this resonance that seemed to provide a form of communication between my left-brain, my right brain, and my blindfolded id. A neutral field of engagement. A common point of view. A triangulated third eye. This added a new dimension to my previously enjoyed two-dimensional world. It was like being given a decoder ring to read between the lines.

Understanding resonance and morphic fields delivered at least the same ninety-seven percent accuracy that I had previously

experienced when I put my faith in a god or a religion. I began once again to rebuild my results-oriented inertia as I learned more about these neutral playing fields surrounding myself. Decoding became an integral part of my life. Finding order within chaos. Patterns from within randomness. Much like the crossword puzzle spelling homework that my girls would bring home from school. Looking crosswise, vertically, horizontally or backwards. I found riddles and back masked messages in the alphabet soup of the visitors that seemed drawn to my home.
These riddles and messages were easily interpreted with the assistance of Janet, which is short for Janet Lee, which is short for Janet Lee Syrup.

Years ago I had seen a character in a movie make a rather nice bong out of a honey-bear squeeze bottle. So, taking my lessons from Hollywood, I found the next best thing in my food pantry, a Janet Lee Syrup bottle. I cut the handle, then heated up the neck with a cigarette lighter and bent it backwards. I inserted a stem and bowl into the cut handle, and voila, I began a close relationship with my friend Janet. Janet was on the guest list for every party and gathering. She was always so easy to get along with and never complained, not even a little. She seemed to know something about most everything. Janet, was also my mother's name. The one, inspiring me to find myself, the other inspiring me to lose myself. To chase coy forty-fives.

"Start them young," she taught,
"Or they'll ask too many questions."

So, in other words, if deceit begins at a young age, say perhaps four-thousand years ago, with floods, serpents, ribs, arks, whales, sacrifices (lots of them), strange porridge, pillars of salt, then many fewer questions will get asked when additional deceit is added such as sea splitting, rams in thickets, boys slaying giants, girls laying with their drunk fathers, mothers telling their children that shepherds are just better than farmers. Mothers with their magical uteri mothering nations. Fathers, slaying their young boys, who may eventually have slain giants. Rams (lots of them), having their throats slit by wandering shepherds. Peaceful farmers having their land inherited by wandering rams, followed by wandering shepherds, slitting the throats of peaceful farmers. Whole families at the same time. Men. Women. Children.

...And back to the magical uteri. Using grade school mathematics, if you take six-hundred thousand boys of fighting age, plus six-hundred thousand girls also of that age, you get one million-two-hundred thousand children of fighting age. Plus, youth of all ages, plus older men and women not able to fight, and you end up with two-million people leaving Egypt on a camping trip. All from just a few hundred magical uteri over a four-hundred-year period. Do the math. The magical bones from the magical offspring of the magical uteri, just vanished. Tripping over the bones of Lucy, dated to over three-million years old, we seem to have a dickens of a time finding any of the two-million bones in the Sinai, supposedly just a few thousand years old. None.
And this deceit was grand-fathered into the stories of Jesus.

Another daughter (in-law), sleeping with her father (in-law), which is OK in this story if it is to preserve good seed.

Like Father, like Son. Or, like father-in-law, like daughter-in-law. Traveling to their Egypt. Their Vegas. Their Dubai. And you know, what happens in Vegas does NOT stay in Vegas. The story multiplies. Like so many sons and daughters. Or like little fishes. Like little loaves of bread. And within minutes, what happened in Vegas, leaves Vegas. All eager to share the Coca-Cola recipe with the world.

"It was six-hundred thousand warriors"

"And they crossed on dry ground"

"He walked on water"

"He healed sick people"

"He cursed a tree"

"He earned that guy Judas
thirty pieces of silver"

He said, to "Come follow Me."

… Oh, and all of the other fire-spinners, hula hoopers, new agers, and drum circlers, into the equivalent of their Black Rock desert. An ancient Burning Man festival. Their gift from God, but only for special people.

The voices,.

…"Leave nothing alive that breatheth when you occupy the gift I am giving you. Not a single trace left behind. Not from man, women, or child."

Deceit, swallowing stories, swallowing more deceit.

These same deceits were also grandfathered into the Holy Roman Empire, into the head of Emperor Constantine, and into the heads at the councils of Nicaea and Trent. Into the searing heat of the Holy Inquisitors savory hot coals. And into the sleight of hand that has now burnished the stories of the bible into the minds of two-year-olds worldwide. And into the minds of adults, acting like two-year-olds worldwide.
And nobody asks any questions, or feels deceived. Why? Because,

"We got to them while they were young."

18

Firewalking and masters of illusion.

Back to these visitors. They included meeting a peculiar friend named Todd, not long after what seemed like lifetimes at the Belvedere. Todd was a Robinhoodesque tax accountant I met who specialized in learning from the rich to benefit the poor. He knew more loopholes than there were lines in the law to put them between. His list of titles included that of being a master hypnotist, and a master of about everything from Reiki to Kabbalah.

●●●

I remember once attending a workshop Todd conducted on positioning assets. His cordless microphone allowed him to diagram his thoughts with one hand on the dry-erase board. His other hand, for lack of an eraser, he was using to wipe the board clean between ideas. Now, watching Todd present a seminar was always a treat. His ideas were always unique and entertaining. So were his nervous twitches, which included blowing into his sweaty palms to keep them dry, wiping his forehead repeatedly, and swiping a finger down his cheek or across his chin in a nervous pattern.

As I sat, mesmerized by his exacting knowledge of formidable loopholes, I noticed that he seemed to be getting pale. More so with each passing moment. His eyes were getting dark and hollow. The person next to me noticed also. I became increasingly concerned that he might soon faint or toss his dinner right in front of everyone. Whispers could be heard throughout the room, I presume from others who also noticed his condition worsening.

Just when I decided to stand up and give him a diversion, he decided to give us a fifteen-minute break. I approached him to ask if he was alright. His ghostly illusion unveiled itself as I discovered that he had unknowingly been face-painting himself. His eraser hand had been ever to slowly adding dark shadows to his forehead, chin, nose and cheeks. Transforming his face, ever so subtly, into a gaunt and hollow expression. He was a true master of illusion.

Eventually, Todd introduced me to a fellow hypnotherapist and master firewalker, Haman. The coals of enticement had gathered for me to receive an invitation to watch some students of theirs participate in a real fire walk. Now, I am a curious cat, but I had seen too much National Geographic TV to even consider dancing my western ass into a bed of glowing coals. I told Todd I would be glad to come and watch. He responded by suggesting that I do a fast the day of the event, adding that many spectators end up walking the fire in the heat of the moment.

On the day of the event, I skirted his advice by picking up fully loaded deli sandwiches on my way to the mountain retreat. I was trusting that food in my belly would strengthen my determination to remain a spectator. It didn't work. Never one to avoid a challenge, I took part in the three-hour preparatory meditation and breath work. A huge mound of split logs fifteen feet long had meanwhile transformed itself into a mountain of hot ambers. We gathered around red-hot coals while the fire tender used a long rake to spread the mass out. I felt the scorching heat of my blue jeans pulled against my skin. Backing away from the heat, I followed Haman's instructions to roll up my pant legs. This was done, of course, to prevent them from catching fire. God! I thought. Forget the pants; what about my feet? I was determined to find a way out, but there were half a dozen women in the group, including a pregnant mother, and my ego noticed that none of them were even flinching.

We formed a fifty-foot circle around the coals. Haman started guiding us into our final mind-over-matter meditation.

> "Cool soft snow."
> "Cool soft snow."

Through squinted eyes, the heat and the ambers seemed to roll and boil like hot lava. "No fucking way!" I thought. I hoped someone else would chicken out first. Haman gave me my hoped-for way out. "Is there anyone who feels like they can't walk this fire?" My hand went up, …immediately (after the woman's hand across from me). For some reason, I felt like I needed his permission to choose out. To bail. The others appeared to be ready, or lying to themselves, or both. My curiosity hoped he would come over, snap his fingers, and say something like, 'On the count of three, you will safely…' Instead, he walked over, stood directly in front of me and asked why I felt that I couldn't walk the fire.

> "I don't trust that I'll be alright."

I replied. With that he snapped his fingers in front of my face, at the same time saying, "Go back to the very first time you didn't trust yourself to be alright." "What are you doing?" Immediately, I remembered being pressed up against a fence by a man. I remembered his cologne; I remembered feeling helpless. "How old are you?" "Seven or eight." Snapping his fingers in my face again, he said,

> "Put yourself right now
> in front of that little boy."

I felt an overwhelming electric feeling tingle all throughout my body. And I was back there. In front of that man, with a little boy behind me. I felt a sensation of floating. My mind was back there; my body was here. I was somehow in both places at the same time, and both places were very real. He next looked directly into my eyes and said,

> "Is anything going to happen
> to that little boy?"

I felt electricity coursing through my body and out through every hair follicle as I replied,

NO!!!

"Do you trust yourself to walk that fire

without being burned?"

"Yes"

I said. Knowing, absolutely, (really?) that I would walk and not get burned.

You can call it trance, hypnotic suggestion, mind over matter, whatever. Hell, you could even say you saw a program on TV claiming that the surface temperature of coals used in fire walking is not hot enough to burn a human. But I was there. I felt the heat. And, for a moment, I was willing to walk across the coals. For me. For that little boy. One small step…, yet one giant leap for my budding consciousness.

I stepped up to the coals just behind Todd, who, for personal fears to overcome, wanted to be the first. Off he went. No drum roll. No tricks. His feet sinking deep into the bed of ambers. He was now on the other side, stepping off onto a slab of cool grass that had been placed there. No screaming. No apparent damage. A moment later, I reached my foot out into the air in front of me.

I cannot accurately describe the moment of truth. The moment my body weight lurched forward behind my suspended foot, and I felt my center of gravity pass through the point of no return. My left-mind was racing. Consuming my right-brain with all the familiar mantras about what was going to happen to my feet.

•••

I remember stepping to the edge of a cliff above a deep pool of water while hiking a slot canyon in the southwest. I had seen two others jump before me into the narrow pool below. One-one-thousand, two-one-thousand, three-one-thousand, splash. They seemed to hang in midair. Although this cliff was higher than anything I had ever jumped off of before, I felt compelled by my ego to do it. For twenty minutes, I would step to the edge, look, get wheezy, and step back. I wanted to chicken out, but the down climb would also have proven itself equally precarious. Finally, I backed up ten feet. Far enough that I could not look down. Then I ran like hell for the horizon. Oh god, oh god! Leaving myself no way out but down. Falling, pounding heart, in-in-inhale, splash.

•••

Back at the coals, my right brain was anxious to cast itself…over matter. But it wasn't just as simple as tricking myself to jump into a pool of cool water. Mind over matter would leave no room for petty adrenalin rushes this time. My left brain was doing its best to keep me safe. I felt my instinct clinging to survival as my state of being followed my bare foot into the hot coals.

"Aum."

My throat mantra reached for the blessings of the aether Gods as I took two, three, four steps into the Captain-Crunchy feeling coals. Oh my god! Six, seven, eight. Touch down. I reached the safety of the cut sod on the other side of the fire before coming back to the sense of what I was doing. I could smell what I thought was the distinctive odor of burnt flesh. My left-brain wanted desperately to be right. Right about all the fears. Right that I should have backed out. Right that I would burn.

I reached down and felt the bottoms of my feet. Then I actually dared to look at them. Then, at the coals. My feet were baby-soft. Not even a blister. My god, I thought again, as I watched the others follow one after the other. I didn't like that I had doubted my results. I wanted to remember it differently, so I walked back to the beginning and started again. Crunch, crunch. This time, I was more in touch with reality. Less mind over matter, crazed with the desire to protect my inner child. I walked to undo the self-doubts I had just created about my first successful walk.

This time, I felt the heat. Felt that perhaps I had not pushed it far enough away from under my feet. Three, four, five...The coals seemed to lick at my feet, displaying the fury of their heat. Aum. Six, seven, eight. Once again, I reached the safety of the other side. Once again, I looked at my feet, at the coals, back at my feet. Baby soft again. I saw others dance and spin through the coals, kicking up embers as they crossed to the other side. In the euphoria of the moment, I walked once more. Others, true to their free spirits, walked several times more.

I still keep the photos we took of each other, next to the Coke can I tore in half to scoop up some of the burnt coals I saved to show any non-believers, including myself. The spent coals are my Spear of Longinus, my Shroud of Turin. I could have walked on water that day. Turned water into wine. But the only souls I saved were my own bi-pedal ones. The vainglory of saving humanity I would leave to the myths of mankind.

CHOKING GOD

• • •

Saving. Being saved. Now, there's a spurious talent for any willing opportunists. I can just see it now.

...And what do you do for a living?

(I am presented a crisp white calling card. Times Roman credentials).

John H. Doe...
Savior.

How exactly does that work? Does he just show up when I need a friend? Will he be there just for me in times of trouble? Speaking words of wisdom? Is there a retainer? Will I be billed monthly? Or will I be forever in his debt? And what about pre-existing conditions?

It's interesting to see how many Christian believers the world over live lives of indebtedness to a savior they've never even met. The supposed saving services that they seem indebted to him for, were deniably rendered hundreds of years ago under very questionable auspices. Not a shred of contemporary evidence for an event that neatly paid a debt for billions and billions of people. Multiply that debt by the thousands of 'wrong doings' each person does in his or her lifetime, and you arrive at the hefty sum of many trillions of wrong doings. All 'paid for', of course, by one man who must, by now, have one hell of a good credit rating. Robbery, paid in full. Rape, paid in full. Pillage, paid in full. Got caught skimming profits from your employer? No worries. Just tell him the story about the dude two thousand years ago who paid back your debt for you. If he seems puzzled, or asks for proof of payment, just tell him that you accepted that dude as your personal savior and that he has conveniently added everything to his tab. If your employer still complains, have him contact God. God bankrolls the savior's debts and should, being perfect, have the wrongs to your employer adding up in an account named,

'Debts Paid In Full.'

Does this sound ludicrous? And yet people willingly consign themselves to a whimsical, Bob Barkeresque, let's-make-a-deal game show for their souls. And, of course, since their savior is no respecter of persons, and his supposed services were given equally to all, balancing the books is as easy as one, two, or three. But wait a minute! What about two-for-ones in the Hail Mary department? Bargain basement pricing on absolution? The priceless friendship with the local clergyman who, for attendance reasons, passes out thoughts on forgiveness of debts (along with the tithing plate) faster than you can say, den of thieves?

In a world of stark realities, greed being one of them, I find it easy to lump sin, guilt, church attendance and salvation into the same operating programs as extortion, bribery, manipulation, and intimidation. All equal parts of the same dirty bathwater. Greed has repackaged spirituality as religion. Religion as the word of God. And God as father Santa or as the Easter Bunny, with a sleigh or a basket-full of lands or blessings. The dumbing down of the human mind is accomplished so easily when it is tucked in behind the doors of "free" salvation.

The only required collateral for this repackaging being acceptance of the idea that a mythical Jesus is your John H. Doe savior. Or, perhaps, that you wear silly hats, clothing, silly underwear, or that you just keep your eye riveted to the seventy-two virgins that some are promised in paradise. And they are not just any heavenly virgins. The ones promised in the Koran don't even menstruate. Don't go to the bathroom. Don't give you any chores to do. And, even given the seeming, 'pulled-this-out-of-my-ass' nature of all these various requirements, promises, and supposed blessings for thousands of years, there are, to this day, no receipts, no happy customers, no postcards, not even a one-star review.

Billions of potential candidates, millions of potential just, thousands of potential martyrs, hundreds of potential saints, dozens of potential prophets, popes, and priestesses. Yet, just a handful of dubious return-from-tomorrow "tunnel-of-white-light" stories.

I feel this stream of thought drifting a little bit. Let me come about and draw in the sails.
Saving souls is a nefarious, idealistic platitude.
What does a soul look like? Unlike offering a hand, or a hand-out, what would a soul saver reach for?
Since no one really knows for sure, how could anyone save one? Except their own. From their own machinations, and from what they feel they must be saved.

●●●

I remember reading a Christmas story to my

daughters when they were young. I was in the mood, using my story-time-dad voice, snuggled between them on the sofa. Having never read this particular story before, I was well into my character when, halfway through, the story took an unusual turn down memory lane. I almost stopped in my tracks, continuing only because I refused to interrupt the holiday spirit of the moment. Somehow this Santa story had turned the common candy cane into a J for Jesus and the red stripes into blood that he 'spilled' to save us from our sins. I about choked on my own tongue. What next? A wreath as his thorny crown? The chimney as his Pentecostal ascension?

My youngest daughter gave me my needed reprieve. Confused by things that even to a six-year-old make no sense, she asked,

"What does a sin mean?"

Now I ask you, what the hell does sin have to do with Santa and Christmas? Oh yeah, same story, different blood, remember? Motivate by fear so that we'll all be good boys and girls for the fat cat in the sky. All the while filling the coffers of the local priest, shaman or thief in the temple making the profits. If in doubt, follow the money. You'll find it snuggled neatly between guilt and religion. And since my daughters had been taught neither of these, the word sin, naturally abbreviated the Christmas story for them as well.

How can one be saved from sins if they have never been taught to have them in the first place? I've learned that who I am as a person has motivated my girls more effectively than fear or guilt.

We had the best Christmas ever. Our own memory lane. Minus the habituated,

"There were in those days shepherds in their fields."

…Ya…in dire need of a good blood bath to wash away their sins.

19

Salvation, and my nose in his glory's belly.

The mental popcorn of existential salvation assumes that somewhere outside my body is a suitable savior who really gives a shit. Blah, blah, blah.

I remember years ago white-water kayaking with my friends Gaston and Peter. We had exceeded our own expectations that particular year of heavy spring run-off. Testosterone clouded any fears left over from years of perfecting our skills. We were kings of our tantric relationship with water. Pushing ourselves. Tempting fate. A quarter inch of injection molded plastic separating our cocoon-like bodies from the pounding, frothy water and the river bottom. An expert Eskimo-roll with the sweep of a paddle was as essential to life as breathing.

The section of river we had chosen that day was appropriately named "Scrambled-egg bend." As if the natural obstacles weren't enough, the remnants of an old road, including rebar iron, cement blocks and debris, had all been responsibly pushed into the river, perhaps adding to its fury.

Our plan of attack was just basically to make it down this section alive. Choosing anything more specific in this flood-stage run-off was wishful thinking. Just looking at the river made me need to pee half a dozen times. We put on our wet suits, spray skirts, and helmets, and carried our boats to the river's edge.

Peter, the more daring of us, decided he was going to start one-hundred yards upriver in order to run a terribly awesome-looking drop just upriver from Gaston and me. If he were to have an unclean run, the recirculating water of the drop would have made it impossible for Gaston or me to rescue him. We waited with throw-ropes ready just in case. Defying fate as he usually did, Peter expertly maneuvered his boat down the drop and pulled into an eddy while Gaston and I got into our boats. Securing my spray skirt, taking in one last deep breath, I pulled into the current.

The chaotic water had a mind of its own. Forcing me down its path of least resistance, the river digested my intention and quickly became a nightmare. Like a tomcat playing with a field mouse, the raging water batted my boat around. My heart was pounding wildly. Water pounded me from all directions. I couldn't see beyond each standing wave in front of me. Gaston and Peter were out of sight. I had no way of avoiding the nasty recirculating 'keepers' that we had carefully scouted and land-marked before beginning our run.

This is what we came here for. The thrill of pushing ourselves to the max. But this was not one of my better days. I was scared shitless. I wasn't in control, and I wanted out. The current was not easy to get into and proved even more difficult to get out of. Relentless and demanding, the best way to describe the feeling inside my chest is that it was like that 'gasp' feeling when I slip on something. Only it kept on going. An endless inhale.

I was unable to avoid the recirculating hole of water right in front of me. Struggling to get my boat out of the jaws of its forceful backwash, I was flipped over into what felt like a mix-master of angry water. My head slammed into a submerged rock. Shaken, but protected by my helmet, I instantly oriented myself, set my paddle, and rolled back upright. My head came out of the water just enough for me to catch a breath, and then I dropped back into another hole of churning water. I was short of breath as I prepared to roll up again. But this hole did not want to let go. Rolling only part way up, I was flipped back over. I forced my paddle down deep, reaching for currents near the river's bottom that might drag me and my boat out of the hole before I tried once more to roll up. It felt like I was under forever. Allowing the river's current to pull me out of the hole, I reached my paddle to the surface once more, made a long sweep and attempted to roll myself back upright. Making it only halfway up, gasping for air, I was rolled back over.

Now, here is the tricky part. When faced with the prospect of drowning, instinct wants to override everything and just get air into the lungs. It wants me to pull out of my boat and just swim for the surface. Training and skill say, "No, stay with the boat." The Eskimo-roll had become instinctual for me. A vital split-second event that life depended on. Mine had now extended to what seemed like ten seconds, then twenty, which felt like an entire lifetime upside down in raging water. I forced myself to do what kayakers resist at all costs. I reached for the release strap on my watertight spray skirt.

Try to picture this. The whole boat is barely taller than me and not much bigger around. The cockpit is small and difficult to get into.

A neoprene skirt is stretched tightly around my waist and also around the neck of the cockpit. The boat is watertight. In it, I float and can roll up. Out of it, I sank like a rock. It was like being born. As soon as I pulled the skirt, I was sucked out of the upside-down cockpit and into the raging water. Product testing 101. Life vest buoyancy is directly related to the sucking effect of turbulent water.

And here is the point of this story. I wanted like hell to be saved. As my head bobbed above the waves, I yelled for help from my friends. I couldn't see them and had no idea if their runs were going any better than mine. My attempts to frantically kick my legs felt more like slow-motion moonwalking. I thought I was a gonner. What I didn't know was that Gaston was directly behind me in his kayak. The bow of his boat was almost touching my head at one point, he said. I was oblivious to his calls for me to grab his boat. He later told me my screams for help sounded no more than a barely audible plea. With no direct communication between us, he couldn't save me, and I couldn't be saved.

As good fortune would have it, a sharp bend in the river had created an eddy behind a huge boulder. Using whatever energy I had left, I made what seemed like a futile attempt to get to the eddy. The hydraulics of the river did the rest. I found myself slowed by the eddy. My legs felt like lead. I reached as far as I could, clutched onto some debris at the river's edge, and held on. In spite of my wetsuit, the freezing water had numbed my body. I was unable to pull myself out of the river, but I felt like I was slipping back into the current. Slowly, I wiggled my body up the embankment like a beached whale and collapsed on the rocks.

Where, may I ask, was my John Doe Savior? In my closet? Under the tree, with Jesus, next to the sweaters? In other words, completely shrouded in mystery and mothballs. If his Golgothic tree falls over in his forest and no one is there to verify it, then he, his forest and his Golgothic tree are down the river with the bathwater.

Meanwhile, I'm still left to drag my body out of the water, arise, and walk the mile to the car in my own shoes. Oh yes, there was only one set of tracks down the road to my car that day. That's because when I felt all alone and needed help, I was carrying my savior's lazy ass on MY back, and that single set of tracks in the sand was my own.

●●●

I remember camping in the early eighties with a friend of mine named Beth. We had met years previous in high school where she shared a locker next to mine. She was one of the few in our school who wasn't a Sunday-go-to-meeting practicing Christian, which was obvious to those who were. In fact, Bible study was even an off-campus elective class that 'faithful' students could take at the local theological seminary. Although it was optional, few kids dared miss their daily dose of bible study. The smokers, the sluffers, the druggies, the Greeks, and my friend Beth. Yet, contrary to what I was taught to think about 'non-believers,' she struck me as being truly genuine, and as someone I could confide in without being judged. Unlike all the 'big brother' watchful Christians with whom I attended bible study.

We met again later while attending college. During fall break, four of us decided to go to Wyoming's Teton National Park. My friend Brighton and I climbed the Grand Teton and met up later with Melissa and Beth, who had stayed at base camp. One evening, Beth and I had taken a walk and I remember gazing up at the midnight sky. I was astounded to see how many more stars were visible here than in my hometown. Perhaps it was the altitude, or the total absence of man-made light. The whole sky was covered in a sea of stars like I had never seen before. Turning to Beth, I commented,

> "Do you ever wonder how God created all of this?"

Her casual reply was,

> "I don't understand, how you can relate everything to a god."

I was stopped short. Don't understand? Just "a god?" In my mind, I was thinking, "How can you look up at all these stars and not relate EVERYTHING to a God?" THE God. My God? It seemed so obvious to me. Obvious, because I had been taught all my life that there WAS a god, and THAT god had created ALL things. So, naturally, HE (God knows how) created all the stars we were looking at that night. In the ensuing silence, I allowed this fundamental difference to begin unraveling our friendship.

Now, forty years later, having cut my umbilical cord to religion and mythical gods, I look up into that same night sky. I notice now how all things seem to be in a relationship, by degree, one to another. Smaller to larger. Warmer to cooler. Faster to slower. Darker to lighter. My place and relationship with humanity is, by degree, as equally balanced as the movements of the largest stars. Both, susceptible to chaos, yet predictable. Both, acted upon by lesser and greater forces.

I marvel that at one time, forty years ago, I looked up and believed there was one man who had developed all the sciences needed to 'create' this vast wonder. And every time I look at the stars now, I still marvel, and express "my god!" to a complexity of nature that operates at all levels in a delicate state of flux. Not getting too close. Maintaining distances. Not close enough. Not enough energy or mass to separate from some things, yet too much energy to get close to others. On the brink of chaos, yet magnificently bound together by degrees of relationship. By fractions of degrees.

And all elements, all matter, from the infinitely microscopic, to the magnanimous macrocosmic, broken down to its individual building blocks of atoms and sub-atomic matter, is, by its own mother natural self, in relationship to everything else.

And that delicate, miraculous degree to which things relate, or seem not to, teeters on boundaries and necessary chaotic changes to bring to my senses, a retinal, cinematic, Sensurround experience that I labeled, at one point in my life, as having been managed, controlled, created, by some exotic vision of a super-human being that I mythologized as an alpha omega god. (whew!!)

Modeled after my own egotistical human image, of course. Dressed in gender and fashion-neutral robes. And someone taught me that this god is above me. Inside of me. All-knowing. All powerful. That I should be like him and no one else. That I should do exactly as he says. And in my obedient, contrite spirit, I believed.

That story feels like being overshadowed or overpowered.

"I will love you if..."

"I will bless you if..."

"Lean not unto thine own understanding,"

this god says.

A pervasive threat of gnashing teeth, wailing,

and fucking hell for the guilty and disobedient. And get this. Freedom from the subsequent worthlessness and unworthiness comes only through more submission to what he says I should do!!

God! Religion is like being up against a fence, with my nose at his glory's belly.

And for one's viewing pleasure, this God is represented by the local ecclesiastical benefactor, pastor, guru, bishop, rabbi, shaman of your choice, who will gladly usurp monies from the masses in exchange for their humility and contrition. And the monies are given, freely mind you. The current return on investment for tithing or donations is, blue sky.

Go figure, which I have. And I've found religion to be the most lucrative form of extortion known to mankind. All other forms use some kind of force or intimidation to extract monies by deceits or threats.

Coherents to religions, on the other hand, give their monies freely. Gladly. Put that easy money equation into the minds of man, let it fester, for, say, a heartbeat, and bingo! Out pops a big business plan called 'building god's kingdom on earth.' That's all one needs. Come up with a good god-story that curiously happens under unverifiable circumstances.

They must be unverifiable so as not to allow the god to be humanized. Say, for example, like Adam, Gilgamesh, Noah, Jehovah, Osiris, Moses, Jesus, and Adonis.

Promise heaven and everything. Deliver nothing. A totally bad-ass coy forty-five. Watch the impetuous phenomenon in mankind described as the placebo effect, naturally happen. And within time, a belief will form. And the money starts pouring in. And men are tempted to screw their neighbor in the name of trust, faith, belief, righteousness, empty promises. …Or just thirty pieces of something.

20

Le roi mourra.
Or, love my enemy, …kill him if necessary.

I haven't written to you for a while now. Perhaps I needed distance. Safety. Some assurance that the sordid details of my more recent past wouldn't catch up to me. Like the tail being pinned on the donkey's ass. I was certain, in the beginning of my story, that my cynicism would keep you spinning just enough to keep you dizzy. Certain that your disorientation would allow you to play the game, and read along without pinning that tail exactly on me, or on my present reality. Violating my delicate sense of self with your disbelief or judgment.

You see, I've been careful to keep my story safe outside the castle walls of my statute of limitations. Protecting me from the seven-year itch to divulge details from within the interior castle of my more recent past. After all, this is my true memoir. And, unlike my fellow Clintonian presidential bard, I did inhale. Deeply. One thing leading to another. Leading to hallways and a gun and to the beginning of my story.

But I've found along the way that truth is subjective. Like the definition of God, love, hot or cold. And, I've found that in writing my memoir, my truth is the events as I interpreted them. As I experienced them. Not necessarily how they were interpreted by the others in my story.

So, I have hesitated the telling of more recent events, leading up to the gun outside my bedroom door, feeling that I might reveal too narrow a perspective. Or, that perhaps, I might describe details that have not had time to fully reveal themselves.

Kind of like saying, "One day, the president was riding in his car, and someone decided to shoot him." But that leaves out possible conspiracies, petty offenses, secrets, jealousies, lies and the nature of triangulation. The certainty of discovering additional shooters, and additional points of view. Given time.

•••

Take, for example, the double-speak of the antagonist I have yet to introduce you to, whose threat I was addressing by sleeping with a gun in the hallway of my home.
When he said to me things like,

"The king won't be around anymore."
"The king is dead."

"The king is not going to be king anymore."

He may not really have constituted a threat to my life. Even when followed up with something vaguely double-spoken about me,

"Not being in the way" any longer.

Or when he made comments about,

"A hole in the desert."

Or to Dean Koontz, or to being buried in a cube van. Wouldn't that be making too narrow an assumption?

Perhaps. But then, on the other hand, I had been taking mental notes of his alpha male behaviors. A telling glance. A subtle but precisely placed finger to the side of the right eye to mark the scent of his double-speak threats. A mental record that he had a prison record. His absolute defiance of police officers. Accusations that he killed his great Dane or that he made an old troublesome girlfriend "disappear." Or the missing two-hundred-pound granite from my entryway shortly after his release from a frequent visit back to prison. Or to having his girlfriend allude to accessing my young daughter's school records. Or alluding to picking them up from school without permission. Or to wanting to have a blonde, blue-eyed child, like my daughters. Or, seeing what appeared to be shotgun welts on the back of his girlfriend Jamie's legs shortly after their move to a trailer in the desert, to "get off the grid."

Or, what about the time he called me at work from my own home phone, gloating that he had maneuvered his way into my home, while I was at work. On, and on, and on. All this is just the tip of a Titanic iceberg of double-speak threats. Many of his subtle threats were meant to imply that any attempt of mine to get him out of my life would bring me harm. What kind of harm? There is no way to tell, since he was very good at using double speak to keep others and me absent of most evidence of what he was communicating to me.

But no, I have to be fair in saying that all this may just be my narrow point of view. Yet, how do I explain to you his references to double meanings, Dean Koontz, and to how long a person could be kept alive in a buried cube van, without giving you just my narrow perspective?

And, by the way, he did have a cube van. He had 're-acquired' it one late night from his girlfriend's ex-husband, claiming that it was 'collateral.' Taking advantage of the generosity of my ex-wife, he had asked her if he could park it for a few days on the pad next to our home. An unexpected visit by police officers the next morning gave me a clearer picture of the nature of his 're-acquired collateral.'

•••

So here I've been, faced with the dilemma of discovering a way to tell you the rest of my story, given that my story involves people and events who are still in my life. You could say I'm waffling, but how do I write about events and people that I am still connected to by all the ripple effects of my contemporary past?

God! Perhaps I've thoroughly fucked myself. I have forgiven myself and too many other people. Which is a bunch of lies. And they have forgiven or accommodated me, which are also just lies. Lies of accommodation.

Lies of saying things that are for the good of the people. Lying described as forgiving, which means literally giving up on one's self. Forgiving and forgetting. 'Remembering no more' for the good of the All. Living lives of sacrifice, forgiveness, judging not, not remembering, forgetting, hanging on crosses for your fellow men because it's the way of the peaceful warrior. It's really a life of death.

Yeah… someone once said…

"Come follow me,"

…Love me the most, above all others, the very highest. …Deny your life!! Hate father, mother, wife, children, even yourselves. Our first little fascist!

…So the story reads.

But that got him dead.

•••

Fuck it all, anyway! What about living entire lives of 'membering,' Of remembering. And of constructing? Not forgetting. Not forgiving. Is there a way to do that and have it be a good thing? Do it in a way that doesn't say,

"I touched you last?"

Since everything is just points of view, does truth really exist? Is it worth it for me to write about the 'truth' of my point of view? Or, given the benefit of hindsight, do I find more worth in forgiving and forgetting? In avoiding the use of those blame mantras?

You've seen the anti-drug commercial on television that starts out with an empty frying pan, while the caption reads,

'This is drugs,'

(two eggs are cracked into the pan),

"And this is your brain on drugs?"

Only I'm not 'getting the picture.'

I do often get hungry for two eggs when I'm on drugs, but 'memory loss?' Fried brains? If you want to talk about memory loss, the pan is forgiveness, and the fried eggs are someone's brain on forgiveness.

Now, do you get the picture?

•••

Crunch!

The sound of metal to metal. Rivets popping. It was so unexpected that for a moment, the crisp air, smooth turquoise glacier water, and breath-taking granite peaks, diffused my instinctual appetite for survival. The next second, I saw our two metal boats grinding together, where moments before, I had seen the small, vulnerable hand of my five-year-old daughter!

God!!! What the fuck!!! Sam had actually crashed into our boat on purpose!!!

Crunch. Grind. He bashed us again. In the middle of Jackson Lake! No thought for my young daughters. He seemed annoyed as fuck that I had abbreviated his plans earlier that morning.

I had taken down our tent, packed the car, and started for home early, stopping only at the lake to give my girls a boat ride. I knew inside, he didn't want us to make it home. Not me, at least. The previous evening, he had been his most bold with the double-speak around the campfire. I thought he might try something for sure. Brighton, Melissa, Mari and Jamie had left us alone at the fire. My girls were fast asleep.

Earlier that week, Mari and I had decided to take the girls camping in Jackson, Wyoming. We had invited Brighton and Melissa. An invitation to Sam and Jamie was now also the standard.
Sam had become a fixture in Jamie's life. Seeking friendship, or safety, Jamie had made Mari a fixture in her life. Seeking neither, I had become a fixture in Sam's life. As an impediment to Sam becoming a fixture in Mari's life.

Sound confusing? It was. Con fusing. It had all started with a knock at the door. The visitors, remember them? At all hours of the night. And remember Rob, the accountant? Rob's tall, skinny frame filled the door. Behind him was Jamie, an old junior high school friend of Mari's. Behind Jamie was her boyfriend, Sam. The night would end in our cozy 'fireroom', with Sam and Jamie kneeling on the floor at the foot of Mari's lounge chair. Jamie was presenting Sam to Mari in what seemed like a ritual offering. Queen to the King.

Four years had gone by since that night when Sam was presented. Our camping trip in Jackson now put me at another fires edge with Sam, playing an alpha-male chess game with the logs. Earlier that day, we had all made an awkward 'footsie-plagued' ascent of Mount Teewinot. A one-day event that did not require ropes, or much mountaineering skill. Dinner was finished uneventfully.

Conveniently retiring to their tents early, Jamie and Mari had left Sam with me at the fire. Sam had put up his high pony-tail, which often preceded his decorative double-speak. He was confidently pacing the fire, declaring himself King.

He was pacing and decreeing, with painfully obvious double-speak, my end as 'king', whatever that meant.

Repeating his double-speak 'diddy' that,

>'A king would need to die.'

That a king would not be king anymore. Declaring check-mate. And as the double-speak became more and more clunky and less effective than a hammer or an axe, the threats and disclosures became decidedly more direct.

I don't remember what I said to end the conversation. I applaud how effectively one's reaction to threat or fear masks some details and memories, while making most essential, those necessary for one's own basic instincts for survival.

I felt unsafe walking to my tent. When I attempted to describe what had just happened, Mari, half awake, seemed to be indifferently aware of what I was now facing and whispered something into my ear. But now my head was reeling with thoughts of putting distance between Sam and me, and getting my family safely home. I didn't sleep.

After a restless few hours, I started packing, and by dawn, our Jeep was loaded, taking Sam and Jamie by surprise. Melissa and Brighton, also surprised, started packing too. Sam immediately noticed, and he, too, started packing, taking note of the girls asking me if we were still going to go for a boat ride at the lake.

We left for the boat dock without making coffee, and reached the boat marina with enough time to rent a small aluminum motor craft, seemingly by ourselves. So, I was surprised to see Sam, Jamie and their dog arrive at the boat dock shortly behind us. It was disconcerting to me that Brighton and Melissa were not behind them.

Out on the lake, my daughters, oblivious to any potential danger, dangled their hands in the cool turquoise glacier water that splashed up as we skimmed along. I had not taken my eyes off of the docks, knowing we would be closely followed. Sam seemed to be driven by a senseless alpha-male short-sidedness.

This was to be a fun boating experience for my girls, not a reckless pas de deux for a prematurely executed *la mort du roi*. I needed a distraction. Something I learned from a grifter on a street corner in Hell's Kitchen back in the 80's after he deftly tossed his three-card Monte and I less deftly lost to him sixty-dollars.

I noticed a small nearby island that was closer than turning back to the marina. I wanted to be out of the aluminum boat. Of course, Sam also pulled his boat onto the shore nearby, and he and Jamie were quickly distracted by their large dog, Taz, leaping onto the beach. Maybe now I'd have some time to let my

basically instinctual suppositions leap out onto the beach and run, and mark, and sniff.
I wanted time to make a decidedly non-aggressive move. A Hippopotamus Mate. I walked with my girls in the opposite direction, yet I sensed something impending. Like crows circling. With Taz distracting Sam, I turned and quickly led Mari and the girls back to the boat. We were not ten-feet from the shore, when Sam and their Great Dane Taz came running. Taz, who was literally his master's dog, even followed us into the lake. At more than half my weight, and taller than me when standing up, my God, I thought Taz was going to jump into the boat after us. He swam for a moment then the frigid glacier water convinced him to turn around.

Not much was said as our boat made its way back to the boat dock. There were three intertwined perceptions experiencing what was going on. Mine. Mari's. And the girls. And my thoughts were about not being on the same road home together with Sam.

•••

I had chosen an indirect route home, attempting to avoid being followed. Barely an hour past the lake, we found Brighton and

Melissa on the side of the road. I pulled over and found Brighton starring at the engine of his new SUV. He seemed annoyed at the inconvenience, While my mind seemed, convinced that this 'annoyance' was just too convenient. Like quantum physics. And entanglement. Afterall, I had left Brighton and Melissa behind with Sam and Jamie when I left the camp that morning.

…And the cock crowed thrice for my perceptions. There was a likelihood that their car was not meant to follow ours to the lake and back home. I didn't like leaving them again on the side of the road. But I had a very real fear that any further delay might put us in reach of Sam bashing us on the road home, or worse.

•••

I loaded the Mac-90 and placed it against the wall outside my bedroom door, a good vantage point from which to also defend the door to my daughter's bedrooms.

Jesus! Here, in my own home!

…My home from which, late one night, Sam had removed a solid granite fixture in our front yard, as a message that *le roi mourra*.

…My home from which, late one morning Sam had called me at my office, from *my* phone, as a message that *le roi mourra*.

This was the nineties. Pre-cell phone. That meant that Sam was inside *my* house, calling me from *my* phone!

I decided to love my enemy, or to kill him if necessary.

•••

I am not a violent person. It's difficult to put a finger on the trigger of a loaded rifle. Either very heavily laden with wood, or not. I felt heavily laden. But it wasn't until a few more bundles of wood, a few more hikes into the wilderness, a few more fake throws, a few more painfully obvious coy 'forty-fives' that I would finally choke my Gods effectively. Fuck the lemons!

21

A gun, a shovel, and the alphabet soup.

A year had gone by since the Jackson incident. The 'sleeping in the hallway' part with a loaded Mac-90 had lasted a few sleepless nights. As days went into weeks, it was clear to me that these smaller moves were becoming part of a much more entangled gambit. The Hippopotamus Mate was being played back on me!

And there were more late-night transformations. A friend of mine had given someone the five-hundred bucks to pay his way for a transformational three-day training, behind closed doors till four in the morning, hugging familiar strangers. I know what goes on behind those closed doors. ...The slicky sweet c'mons of unconditional love. And boundaries there are for losers. Our phone was once again occupied by Sam, calling in nightly to his team leader. ...Without bounds.

The veneer, separating me from any abbreviations to my reactions, was wearing paper thin.
An unexpected reprieve presented itself. And soon after that, Sam and Jamie lost their

home.

The cube van now came in handy. Believing that perhaps this was a final chapter, I anticipated, with any dust-covered faith and hope, that the stuffed cube van would soon leave town with my antagonist.
On the day of the expected departure, I received a call from the sitter letting me know that my daughters were still waiting to be picked up. What? Very odd. They were always picked up on time. I arrived at the sitter's and began to collect my thoughts. The phone rang.

The cube van had not left town! The cube van was with Sam, and Mari was with the cube van, and the phone call was supposedly coming from a shop where the broken-down cube van was now being fixed. Does this all seem confusing? No. By now, many things were crystal clear.

•••

Months had gone by, and Sam and Jamie were now living off the grid in a trailer they had acquired in the Sierra Nevada desert. Yet that same impending feeling I had, never left. It seemed like an old lid that was screwed on crooked. Like unfinished business. Keeping my friends close, and my enemies closer, the alphabet soup was saying,

"Don't go back; you will kill others."

But I found it was not as easy as simply hanging up a 'closed sign.' I feel that I understand now why many victims seem to place themselves back in proximity to their perpetrators. It feels safer knowing where they are than not knowing. Quantum physics and entanglement just don't recognize those 'closed' signs either. One can't simply unknow some things, or un-participate oneself from some things.

•••

I once watched a documentary about a beautiful octopus. Changing the colors of its pigment instantaneously, like a giant kaleidoscope. Shape-shifting. Simulating the texture and shape of kelp one moment, and then that of dead coral the next. Sensing danger, then collecting shells into its suction cups, to then roll-up inside-out into a ball of sea-shells to avoid being eaten. Amazing! Eating prey with stealthy, sleight-of-hand. Searching the sea-bottom for a snack. ...Being followed by a shark. Perhaps becoming a snack.

The end seemed inevitable. Try as it might, the elegant octopus could not undo itself from its own lingering scent of deliciousness that it left behind unwillingly. Easily followed by the shark's keen sense of smell, even in darkness, the ripping and tearing that followed reminded me that, in order to not wake up with a hang-over tomorrow, I must avoid having too many drinks today. To not be entangled, one must not tangle in the first place. To untangle myself from cube vans, dead kings, popped rivets, and libidinous predilections, well, that was going to take a gun again, and a shovel.

22

You get to keep the shoes.

I was prepared to kill. That would be a fucking lot of digging. And I'm not a violent person. The deepest hole would be last. Of course, after finishing with the car, the tracks, the firepit. I felt it in the air. But for now, we had just started building the fire. And we were making yet another play at 'whose logs were bigger.'

The coy forty-five of this particular trip, into this particular Sierra Nevada desert, into this particular canyon, on this particular turn onto Elm Street, on this particular weekend, was an obviously attempted "Ollie."

You remember, in that childhood game? Only a simple-minded 'Ollie' would 'come in free', if not found by the seeker. Only an 'Ollie' willing to give up his or her best hiding place, willing to give up a safe-haven, would come in free without a plan. Only a simple-minded Isaac would carry wood to a sacrifice, without wondering,

"Where is the sacrifice?"

•••

I have seen this place before. I am certain of it. In the arms of Gaia, once after drinking a warm mushroom tea. It looked far different now from the ground. This canyon. These cliffs. This abruptness. Those green cottonwoods down below. That red rock. The blue sky.

•••

I was prepared to kill. My god. How do I even say that? Yet, unlike Isaac, I did not take wood to a knife fight. Or a knife to a gunfight.

•••

He, uncertain now of his perfectly executed coy forty-five. His painfully obvious attempt at bonding. Me, certain of his uncertainness. She, miscalculating both, but prepared for either. Walking to the edge of the cliff. She, close behind, uncertain. He, steps behind her, calculating my certainty.

•••

The fire. The log comparing again. The 'random' dirt road. The proximity of good cliffs. The apparent bonding of brothers.

After many attempts, many more attempts, and yet several more attempts, even I, too, was able to use a bow and drill to create a tiny ember. Placing the coal into the ball of tinder in my palms, I blew until a grey smoke wafted up from the ember and suddenly burst into flames. Holding up the flame, once again turning vegetation into jubilation, I released the ball of fire into our stack of logs. My face looked like Dick Van Dyke's after a few chimneys.

The next few hours tending the fire were 'footsie-plagued' and tedious. Avoiding the inevitable. And then the hike naturally followed. Figuratively on me, had been placed the faggot of wood. A suitable precipice to serve as an altar was found next. The voices in the heads of the sacrificers had spoken.

> I see mighty Aphrodite
> Fast becoming
> The thoughts that provoke her
> Thoughts that dress and undress
> A thousand breasts
> Slipping layer from layer
> Like the last silk leaflets
> Plucked from an artichokes heart
> To reveal yet another pubic mantra

"Be gone, I conceal the secrets of love"
And torn asunder, raped and plundered
She lays bare the chests of armies
Starves the poor, the meek, the hungry
Bankrupts kings, priests and tyrants
Hews down forests for her palaces
Enslaves silkworms for her wares
Slays the most sensuous of animals
The mink, the sable, the ermine, the fox
To bind their skin around her neck
Their limp seduction hanging
Like her purple heart of valor
Lives given for her life
Streets hewn through rock and chasm
Mountains laid flat, rivers stopped up
To erect high phallic cities
Bigger armies, missiles ejaculating death
And for what?
The game is over, then she cries
"Ollie, Ollie in free"
But no one's coming
"Come out, come out
Wherever you are"
And barren streets echo
The stillness

•••

But…
                No. No. NO!!

On this particular trip, on this particular weekend, into this particular canyon, I was not going to be carrying any wood on my back. And I was not 'coming in free.' And there would be only one set of tracks in the sand. Nothing left to doubt, or to nefarious gods, or to the ninety-seven-percent gamble. In the months leading up to this trip, I had discovered the nakedness of my Aphrodite's, and of my Gods.

I had discovered the muses of my coy forty-fives, and of my simple-mindedness.

•••

My feet, as to an altar, were at the very edge of the precipice. Behind me, inside of me, through me, was that little boy. No gamble. My muses, my Gods, and my Jesus were off somewhere playing with a bunch of marbles at the foot of some crosses, near a pile of nails.

The 'staying of the hand' part was stuffed into a psychological Gordian's knot, which was stuffed into a Schrödinger's box, which was stuffed into my back left pocket. With its safety-off.

Once again, there was no satisfaction for the crowds. No fists were thrown. There was no small print. There was not a 'binding.' No knicks or irregularities suffered to a well-kept chalaf. No rams in thickets of sacrificial gravy standing ready as 'seconds' should the sacrifice have failed. The altar was figuratively and actually avoided. There were no winners. And, significantly, no losers. Nobody on a cross.

There was no 'Eloi, Eloi' begged of my right brain's silliness. My pineal ID had carried me indifferently on its back. Caring only to survive. Adapting to, and gathering information along the way.

•••

The tips of my toes, pretending to keep me from falling. The emptiness pulling me. Daring him. Scaring her. All of us hesitating. Perhaps they, knowing that I knew. Perhaps me, knowing that they knew. My neck hairs poised. Once again. Each one trembling. Knowing that it was NOT emptiness behind me that I was fighting. I would not be waiting for an angel of God to stay this hand. To stay these voices.
The 'happy accident' that had been the fodder for those planning this trip, was now

imminent. I wouldn't last much longer on the edge without simple gravity just pulling me over.

I was, in that moment, prepared to silence voices. To *not* stay the hand. To make use of the 'ritual Chalef, that' I had carefully loaded in each chamber, and brought with me. And, as my hand stood ready to reach for it, I was also conscious that I had come prepared for more than only a knife fight.

And I was, in that moment, my own angel, my own voice. And a fall was avoided. And a hand was stayed. And when the staring and posturing stopped, two hippopotamuses were left staring at each other. And I take pride in my talent, skill, level-headedness, and determination, that had kept the safety latch, …Off. Prepared. At the ready. The one-hundred-percent gamble.
  Three birds in two hands, and none in the bush.

•••

To be unveiled the secrets of a quantum Gordians knot, or the secrets of a Schrödinger's box, one must let them go. Leave the knot tied. Leave the box unopened. Curiosity kills the cat.

Only on our way back down the mountain, when I was certain of my certainty, did I slide the safety, …On. And just like that, my psyche released me again from bondage to my Gods.

•••

Fortunately for me, unfortunately for you, I did not write the ending to this memoir while I was still choking my gods. 'Those' Gods.' When it was I, myself, who needed choking, my god, from all of my gods. And, thank god, that my story is still this side of shovels and digging and pits and guns.

…After all, the digging would have been unbearable.

I am somewhat more indifferent now than I was back then to the specificities of hurts and pains and violent deeds, and to the events of who hit whom first, or is it last?

No doubt you wanted to read my story the way it really happened. You wanted me to remember everything. To not hold back. But what if I've forgiven certain dastardly deeds in my story? Forgotten them? 'Drawn pistols' with them? Is it politically correct in the 'forgiveness world' for me to not forget, and instead to remember these things? Absolutely not! But for this story, I am a liar. I did remember. Some thoughts, some petty details. So, did I really forgive? Hell no! It clearly was always a lie.

I am designed naturally to remember, to record. Naturally, you wanted details, or, like a good liar, I wanted to give you details. Details make life interesting. Details are life. Like triangulation and points of view. I wanted to give you the grassy knoll version of my story and uncover for you all the mysterious additional shooters. I wanted to show you the Zapruder tape of my life, complete with me crawling down the back of my topless limo, scooping up for you handfuls of my brain matter. The Camelot of my tidy relationship racing off under the watchful eyes of my very friends who wanted to fell it.

However, all the hands in my story are bloodied and guilty. Including mine. So, some key details I have intentionally left out. A mild Chappaquiddick whitewashing.

If you liked this 'Warren Report' version of my story,

'…a single shooter,'

'…what apple?'

…Then perhaps, in time, another story will be told with additional facts and relevant points of view.

For now, I have given you a story that does not unnecessarily raise the ire and silencing hands of the 'Sirhans' who might wish to keep certain things in my story silent.

•••

Me, I am getting my marbles back. I am choking my relationships to my gods. Wringing their beady little necks. Dancing barefoot before my own magnificent burning bush. Listening to the commands of my own mouth and heart.

My own holy self, expressing my own miraculous being.

●●●

I still keep on my bookshelf, a convenient little sandbag of course. Attached to it is a hand-written note that reads, in very, very, small print.

"You get to keep the shoes."

With love,
the Muses.

www.ingramcontent.com/pod-product-compliance
Lightning Source LLC
Chambersburg PA
CBHW041304110526
44590CB00028B/4240